Sleeping on the Wing

Sleeping on the Wing

An Anthology of Modern Poetry
with Essays on Reading and Writing

Kenneth Koch
and Kate Farrell

VINTAGE BOOKS

A DIVISION OF RANDOM HOUSE

NEW YORK

*Grateful acknowledgment is made to the following for permission to reprint
previous published material:*

Georges Borchardt, Inc.: "The Instruction Manual" and "The
Painter" are reprinted from *Some Trees* by John Ashbery (published by
Holt, Rinehart & Winston). Copyright © 1962 by John Ashbery. All rights
reserved. Reprinted by permission of the author and Georges Borchardt,
Inc.

City Lights: "Howl Part I" from *Howl and Other Poems* by Allen
Ginsberg, copyright © 1956, 1959 by Allen Ginsberg. Reprinted by
permission of City Lights Books. "The Day Lady Died" from *Lunch Poems*
by Frank O'Hara. Copyright © 1964 by Frank O'Hara. Reprinted by
permission of City Lights Books.

Editions Gallimard: "La Petite Auto" ("The Little Car") by
Apollinaire Guillaume, copyright © Editions Gallimard 1959. Reprinted by
permission of Editors Gallimard.

Harcourt Brace Jovanovich, Inc.: "The Love Song of J. Alfred
Prufrock" and "Preludes" from *Collected Poems 1909–1962* by T. S. Eliot,
copyright 1936 by Harcourt Brace Jovanovich, Inc., copyright © 1963,
1964 by T. S. Eliot. Reprinted by permisison of the publishers.

Harvard University Press: Seven poems by Emily Dickinson are
reprinted by permission of the Publisher and the Trustees of Amherst
College from *The Poems of Emily Dickinson,* edited by Thomas H. Johnson,
Cambridge, Mass.: The Belknap Press of Harvard University Press,
Copyright 1951, © 1955, 1979 by The President & Fellows of Harvard
College.

Alfred A. Knopf, Inc.: "Disillusionment of Ten O'Clock," "Thirteen
Ways of Looking at a Blackbird," "Depression Before Spring,"
"Metaphors of a Magnifico," "Ploughing on Sunday," and "Gubbinal,"
copyright 1923 and renewed 1957 by Wallace Stevens; "Anecdote of the
Jar," copyright 1923 and renewed 1951 by Wallace Stevens; "The Brave
Man," copyright 1936 and renewed 1964 by Holly Stevens; "A Rabbit as
King of the Ghosts," copyright 1942 by Wallace Stevens and renewed
1970 by Holly Stevens; "Anecdote of the Prince of Peacocks," copyright
1923 and renewed 1951 by Wallace Stevens. All poems are reprinted from
The Collected Poems of Wallace Stevens by Wallace Stevens, by permission of
Alfred A. Knopf, Inc. "A True Account of Talking to the Sun at Fire
Island," copyright © 1968 by Maureen Granville-Smith, Administratrix of
the Estate of Frank O'Hara; and "Poem: Hate Is Only," copyright © 1960
by Maureen Granville-Smith, Administratrix of the Estate of Frank O'Hara.
Both poems are reprinted from *The Collected Poems of Frank O'Hara* by
Frank O'Hara, by permission of Alfred A. Knopf, Inc.

Liveright Publishing Corp.: "my sweet old etcetera" from *IS 5,* poems
by E. E. Cummings, copyright 1926 by Horace Liveright, copyright
renewed 1954 by E. E. Cummings. "somewhere i have never
travelled gladly beyond" from *ViVa* by E. E. Cummings, copyright 1931,
1959 by E. E. Cummings, copyright © 1979, 1973 by Nancy T. Andrews,

Library of Congress Cataloging in Publication Data
Koch, Kenneth, 1925–
Sleeping on the wing.
Bibliography: p.
Includes index.
1. Poetics.   2. Poetry, Modern.
I. Farrell, Kate.   II. Title.
PN 1042.K55   1981b   808.81'03   80-5278
ISBN 0-394-74364-4   AACR2

Manufactured in the United States of America

Cover art by Red Grooms

D9876543

TO DAN AND SHANE FARRELL

Acknowledgments

A few years ago, Michael Spring commissioned a series of reading-and-writing essays on modern poems for *Scholastic*'s magazine *Literary Cavalcade*. Some of these essays, which first appeared in the magazine and in a *Scholastic* anthology, were early versions of essays in this book; and it was doing these first essays that gave us the idea to do such a book. We thank Michael Spring. And Myra Klahr of the New York poets-in-the-schools program, who found high school classes in which we could try out the teaching ideas presented here. And the students in Kate Farrell's classes at Garden City High School, Valley Stream High School North and Valley Stream High School South, and the students in Kenneth Koch's classes at Columbia University, where we tried the ideas out. And for other invaluable assistance we thank Gary Fisketjon, Carolyn Lumsden, and John Sterling.

Contents

Sleeping on the Wing

Introduction

This is an anthology of modern poetry. It includes a number of pages of poetry by each poet who is in it, and has essays about the poets and their poems and suggestions to you for writing poems of your own. Because of various misconceptions about how poetry is supposed to be written and read, many people avoid poetry during their education and afterward—they get the idea that poetry is for a few people with special poetic sensibilities. And they miss a great deal. Reading poetry and writing poetry are natural and worthwhile and pleasant things to do. You will find that reading poetry is a great help in writing it, and that writing it is very good for your understanding of what you read. A logical place to start reading poetry is with modern poetry—since that is the poetry of our own time. It is also a good place for people who are writing now to find inspiration for their own poems.

THE POETS IN THIS BOOK

This book includes poets who have written in English from the middle of the nineteenth century until now—

from Walt Whitman to Frank O'Hara—as well as some of the best modern poets who have written in other languages—Rimbaud and Apollinaire, from France; Lorca, from Spain; Rilke, from Germany; Mayakowsky, from Russia. You'll find in it a great variety of poetic styles, of themes, of ideas of what poetry is.

This book is arranged so that all of a poet's poems are together. There's enough of each poet's work to help you start getting to know it. Sometimes before they know much about poetry, people have the idea that all poetry is more or less the same—a way of writing about special poetic subjects in a certain poetic way. This would make poetry rather uninteresting if it were true, but it isn't.

Every good poet has an individual and original way of writing. When you first read a poet's work, that originality will be part of what makes it seem strange and unfamiliar. It's something like what happens when you go to a foreign country. It's possible to find the strangeness exciting right way. Of course, what's strange can also be confusing at first and can make things seem difficult.

Accompanying each poet's work in this book is a short essay about the poet and the way he writes. This will help you to become familiar with the poet's style, help you see the point of writing that way, and in general give you a way to begin to feel at ease with reading the poems. After a while you can get to know the styles of various poets, the way you know the personalities of your friends or the sounds of different musical instruments. You will probably like some poets better than others and will be able to think about the differences and talk about your own ideas.

The poets in this book were chosen because they're all very good poets and because their work has proved to be interesting and inspiring to students. Sometimes there are more poems from the early part of a poet's career—it is often the poems written when a poet is young that are closest to a student's experience. Sometimes it is in a very long poem that a poet is at his best. In a few cases selections from such long poems have been included. In the essays there is some discussion of individual poems, but of course there is no attempt to explain or analyze everything. There are also suggestions about ways to write poems inspired by the poet's work.

If you like poetry, you'll probably find poets who are not in this book whose work you like a lot. If you like a certain poet who is included, you will probably want to find his books so that you can read more of his work. This book is meant to be only an introduction, a beginning.

MODERN POETRY

Poetry is different in different times. What people experience is different and so, to some extent, is the language they use. Think about Shakespeare's English. Taking a walk in sixteenth-century London was different from what it is to take a walk there now, and the way people thought about taking a walk there was different, and the kind of poem anyone would write about taking a walk was different too. And despite the differences in poets' styles, there is something that can be recognized as the style or way of writing of a particular historical period. The other arts, too, change in this way.

Poets are inspired by what the world around them is like. Because that changes, poetry changes. They also have a desire for their poetry to be different from any that exists so far. That also makes poetry change. And so the best poetry of a particular time often seems strange or puzzling to the people of that time because it has been affected by these changes and, as a result, is different and people aren't used to it yet, although later it may not seem strange or puzzling at all.

Modern poetry is probably as different from what came before it as any poetry has ever been, which, if you think about the enormous changes that have been brought about in our time by science and technology—changes in transportation and communication, for instance—is not completely surprising. There is so much new knowledge—and a new idea, too, of the vastness of what is still left to discover and know. It would be strange if that hadn't affected people's thinking about everything, including poetry.

Modern poets have tried a great variety of forms, new ways of putting words together, of punctuating, of beginning and ending, of dividing up poems. And they have been more interested in nonrational ways of thinking than most poets before them—interested in dreams, in the unconscious, in accidental inspiration. They have tended to avoid the usual forms, the usual ways of saying things, the usual ideas, the logical connections, anything that might be limiting. Sometimes their poems seem almost like a new language.

Change and newness are part of what poetry is about (and they are an important part of what much modern poetry is about), and part of what makes it exciting and worth reading. Once you see that, the surprisingness of modern poetry won't get in the way of your liking to read it.

READING POETRY

The experience you get from reading poetry is not exactly like any other. Sometimes poetry gives the impression of saying more than words can say. This mysterious-seeming effect is caused by the fact that in poetry words are used in a way that is different from the way words are usually used. Poetry is art, and so has a different purpose from that of the regular way of talking and writing, and has a different effect.

Most of the difficulties that people have in reading poetry come from their not understanding this. It is easier to understand using a rock to make sculpture, or sound to make music, than it is to understand using words to make poetry. Words already have meanings and ways of being put together to get something across. So, when you read words, it is natural to expect the ordinary kind of intellectual sense that you are used to, a kind of sense you don't expect, for instance, when you listen to music. Once you understand what poetry is and how it is different from other writing, it won't seem to you so confusing and difficult.

Usually when you talk or write, you start with an idea, then try to express it in words and in a style that will make it clear to the people you are talking or writing to. Sometimes that's easy. You say, "I would like a glass of water." Sometimes it's hard. Talking about strong or complicated feelings—about being in love, for instance, or feeling sad—you may end up with a feeling that you haven't really said what you meant, that there isn't any way to put what you feel into words. The more personal the thing that you want to say, and the more particular it is to your own way of thinking and feeling and seeing things, the less likely it is that you can express it with the ordinary way of talking.

Suppose you decide to find a way of talking in which you can express perfectly your own sense of things, your thoughts or way of seeing, or your own particular experience. And that it becomes more important to you to get those things right than to make sure somebody else understands them. Suppose you want to get an experience into words so that it is permanently there, as it would be in a painting—so that every time you read what you wrote, you reexperienced it. Suppose you want to say something so that it is right and beautiful—the way music is right and beautiful—even though you may not understand exactly why. Or suppose words excite you— the way stone excites a sculptor—and inspire you to use them in a new way. And that for these or other reasons you like writing because of the way it makes you think or because of what it helps you to understand. These are some of the reasons poets write poetry.

It doesn't make sense to read poetry the way you read a newspaper article. It is good, in general, to read a poem with the kind of freedom, openness and sensitive attentiveness to your own thoughts and feelings that you have when you write a poem yourself or when you listen to a friend talking, or when you hear music. You understand the meaning of the words in the poem with your intellect, but you also respond to the poem with a part of your intelligence that includes your feelings and imagination and experience.

You can like a poem before you understand it, and be moved by it, and in fact, that is a sign that you're starting to understand it, that you're reading the poem in a good way. Being moved by a poem—laughing or feeling sad or full of longing—or being excited by it, or feeling (maybe you don't know why) the "rightness" of the poem is a serious part of reading and liking poetry. You may find what you read to be beautiful, or be reminded of places and times, or find in it another way to look at things. All this can help you to understand the poem because it brings it closer to you, makes it a part of your experience. And the better you understand a good poem, the more you'll like it.

The best way to begin is by reading the poem several times to get used to the style. After you get a sense of the whole poem, there are some things you can do to help yourself understand anything that's unclear—if anything still is unclear, which often it won't be. There may be a word or two you don't understand, or a reference to a person or a place that you're not familiar with. These you can look up in a dictionary or encyclopedia or ask someone about. There may be a sentence that's so long it's hard to follow, or a sentence that's left incomplete; words may be in an unusual order, or a sentence may be hard to see because it's divided into different lines. For these problems, just go through the poem slowly, seeing where the different sentences begin and end. If you understand part of a poem and not another part, try to use what you do understand to help you see what the rest means.

If the poem still seems hard to you, it may be because you're looking for something that isn't there. You may think that the poem makes a point, that it comes to some conclusion about life in general, when the point may only be to get into that poem the look of a locust tree in the early spring. Or you may be looking for a hidden meaning that isn't there. The suggestiveness of poetry often makes people think there is one specific hidden meaning. There isn't one. A good poem means just what it says, and it suggests what it suggests. The search for deep meanings behind what is said is usually painful and unrewarding. Poems don't usually have hidden meanings. One main trouble with "finding" such meanings when they're not really there is that they end up hiding what really is there. One of Wallace Stevens's poems begins

> The houses are haunted
> By white nightgowns.

He means, in fact, as you realize after you read the poem a few times and get to know it, that people are wearing conservative white night clothes which make them look like ghosts. It's a witty way of making fun of them for being so conservative and dull. If you start off looking for hidden meanings, however, you may never know this. You may start thinking of a supernatural phenomenon, of real ghosts, maybe even of Lazarus and his rising from the grave, and you'll lose the poem completely. It's like looking for the real meaning behind a sailboat race on the bay. You'd probably miss the beauty and excitement of the boats, the water, the sky, the day. Remember (writing poems of your own will help you to know it) that poets are not big, dark, heavy personages dwelling in clouds of mystery, but people like yourself who are doing what they like to do and do well. Writing poetry isn't any more mysterious than what a dancer or a singer or a painter does. If a poet writes well, what he says is to be found in the words that are actually there, almost always in the commonest meanings.

Sometimes, too, people make the mistake of analyzing the poem word by word before they've got an idea of what the whole poem is like. This seems scholarly and scientific but is as misleading as analyzing each of a person's words in a conversation before you know who he is and what he is talking about. Better than starting right in to analyze according to some already existing idea is to think of how the poem is affecting you, think of your own responses to it. Also, when first reading a poem, you don't have to be concerned with its technique, with how it is made—that is to say, its rhyme, its meter, its imagery, and so on. That can be interesting to talk or write about later, but when you're first reading a poem you don't need to do it.

Even when they don't know much about poetry, people sometimes have strong ideas about what poetry ought to be like. This can keep them from enjoying all the different ways poetry can be. If you read poetry expecting it to be always the same, you will be confused. It is an art, like music or painting, with all kinds of possible variations.

Everything you like about a poem will be enhanced, and what you understand of it will be increased, by reading other poems by the same poet. As you get used to a poet's style and so on, you can hear everything in his poems more clearly. If you don't feel intimidated, understanding or figuring things out can be enjoyable in itself. Think of the rather pleasant process of figuring out a part of town you've never been in or an interesting person you've just met.

Reading poetry is not a completely passive pleasure, as is sitting in the sun or watching television. It is more like the pleasure you get from playing tennis or listening to music. There is a difference between what you feel the first time you play tennis and the fiftieth time. Or between the first time you go to a concert and later on, when you know more about the music and are used to concerts. Poetry is like that. The more you know about it and the more you read it, the more at ease you'll feel with it, the better you'll get at reading it, and the more you'll like it. When you read a poem, the poet's experience becomes, in a way, your own, so you see things and think things you wouldn't see and think otherwise. It's something like traveling—seeing new places, hearing things talked about in new ways, getting ideas of other possibilities. It can change you a little and add to what you know and are.

TALKING ABOUT POETRY

Poetry is there to be read. It's fine to read it privately and in silence, to enjoy it, to think about it, to understand whatever you understand. Most reading is like that, as is most looking at art and listening to music. Still, when you feel strongly about a poem or any other work of art, it's natural to want to talk about it, to say what you think, to make your ideas about it and your opinion of it clear to other people. However, it is one thing to understand something, another to be able to talk about your understanding. Putting ideas into words so that others can understand what you mean is sometimes hard, but, like other things, with practice it becomes easier. And doing this kind of talking, or writing, about a poem makes you begin to understand the poem better yourself, makes you know more clearly what it is that you think.

There is no one right way to talk about all poetry. Talking about all poetry in the same way makes no more sense than talking, for instance, about all sports in the same way. You admire different qualities, you watch for and are excited about different things, you even use different terms, when you look at soccer and when you look at baseball. And, of course, you only find out how to talk about all that by watching the games. In something like that same way, you find out how to talk about the work of different poets by reading it and by thinking about what makes it the way it is, what makes it, for example, different from the work of other poets that you have read. If you concentrate on the poem instead of on some general idea about poetry, you'll have a better chance of talking about it in an interesting and intelligent way.

If a poem is long and rambling and has hundreds of details, you don't pay as much attention to each word as you do if it is a thirteen-line poem with only one word in each line. In discussing William Carlos Williams's short poem about the red wheelbarrow, you might want to talk about the unusual way the lines are divided up. It wouldn't be as interesting to do this with most poems by Yeats, for example. And it would be absurd to talk about Williams's poem as one might of one of Yeats's, looking for extra meanings behind the words—supposing, for example, that the word *white* (in Williams's phrase "white/chickens") suggests purity and innocence.

The idea behind talking about poetry is not to get to the bottom of it, but to clarify it, to make it more a part of what you and other people know and will remember. Sometimes people think that they must be able to talk about the "real meaning" of a poem, by which they mean some truth they think must be behind it. But there isn't such a truth. A poem is all its words and music and lines and meanings, and it can't be reduced to some single truth any more than can a novel or a symphony or a statue. If a statue could be reduced to, say, "friendship" or "the love of nature," you wouldn't need the statue, with all its curves and angles, the smoothness and color of its stone, the weight of its shoulders, the gesture of its hand. Sometimes you may get a strong insight into a poem, and this can seem like its whole meaning. But if you keep on reading the poem, and talking about it, you'll probably get other insights too, which will also be part of the meaning.

What a poem makes you feel helps you make sense of it by making the poem part of your own experience. What it makes you feel, of course, can be affected by what you're feeling at the time you read it: you may be sad, happy, in love, afraid; or you may be preoccupied by certain thoughts. It's hard to tell sometimes whether it's the poem that's sad or whether you are sad, in which case almost any poem might seem sad to you. When you're talking about a poem and aren't sure if something is in the poem or mainly in your feelings, it's all right to say "I think" or "It seems to me." In general, it's always best not to go too far in interpreting something in a poem—you don't have to reach conclusions. If a poem seems to you to have a dreamy quality, it's not quite true to say that it has a dream in it. It's better to say exactly why you think the poem is dreamlike: "The poem moves from one thing to another in an unexpected way, the way dreams do."

In talking about a poem, don't feel you have to say everything. It is good to be able to say a few things clearly. You'll do it best if you feel free and unembarrassed, the way you feel when you talk to friends. The ideas you'll have about poetry, like ideas about other things, may be vague at the start and get clearer only while you are talking about them. When you do get something right, it's a pleasure—when you can make something clear and understandable that before seemed hard. Make what you say as simple as you can, and be specific and give examples to show what you mean. Sometimes because they find poetry difficult and complicated, people make the mistake of talking or writing about it in an abstract, general, overcomplicated way. They think that being abstract and general is more serious and is the way to talk about difficult and important things—that being simple means you're "shallow" or uncomplicated or unintelligent. In fact, abstraction is often a way of being evasive and can hide what you do know. Being simple is sometimes hard, but it's worth it. Ezra Pound's poem "The River-Merchant's Wife: A Letter" is about a young wife's longing for her husband to come back home to her; she is lonely and feels she is changing. If you said, "On one level this poem is about time and mortality," that wouldn't tell anyone much about the poem, not nearly as much as if you said, "Time is passing and the young wife is growing older."

To be convincing, you need to refer to particular parts of the poems—that is, to words and lines. Quoting is an essential part of making things clear. Say that you're talking about William Carlos Williams's poem "Nantucket." One thing you might say is that everything is described as it would be seen by someone actually inside the room in the inn in Nantucket. For example, the flowers outside are seen from inside, with their colors slightly different because of the curtains. To make this clear, you'd quote from the poem:

Flowers through the window
Lavender and yellow
Changed by white curtains . . .

Sometimes when you write a paper or discuss a poem, you'll be talking about poems you already know and have thought about. At other times, in a class, you may be asked to talk about a poem you've just read or don't completely understand or don't know yet if you like or not. This is harder. Go slow, be simple and clear, and say how it seems to you and what exact words and lines in the poem your ideas and feelings come from. If asked what you think about a poem, say anything about it that seems to you interesting and, if you can (it's very difficult sometimes), why. Don't be afraid to be critical of poetry—there's nothing sacred about it. Also, don't hesitate to say when you don't understand a poem or some part of it. Even if you don't understand it, you can talk about its tone (does it sound like something you'd hear in church? at a party?), the kinds of words in it, its title, how things are connected in it, how it begins and ends. Don't expect to be completely clear right away. In classrooms, not being able to explain clearly what you are thinking, or not knowing everything about something, can make you feel stupid. Try not to let it. Start anywhere. Practice will make you good at this kind of talking, and it is satisfying to be good at it. Once you know a few poems by the same poet, you can talk about how a particular poem is like or unlike his other poems, or how his work is like or unlike that of another poet.

USING THE WRITING
SUGGESTIONS IN THIS BOOK

Writing poetry is interesting and exciting. Why would poets write it if it weren't? But writing poetry for a classroom assignment often seems difficult and boring and embarrassing. Students think that they won't write well enough, that they won't be able to get started writing—to find a first line, to find something to write about, to find enough to say. They're afraid that they won't be inspired, that they have no ideas that are right for poetry. One reason for this difficulty in writing poetry is probably that the way many people think that poetry should be written has been very much influenced by various old-fashioned and false ideas about poetry—ideas that can make poetry writing seem like an unrewarding struggle. The writing suggestions in this book, suggestions which are largely inspired by what has happened in modern poetry, should help you to be free of useless worries and constraints, and to write in somewhat the way other modern poets have written.

And so the poems you write are likely to be different from the ones you have written before. And the way of writing may seem different from the way you thought poems were written. But you will probably end up liking to write and liking your poems.

At the end of each essay about a poet's work is a suggestion (sometimes more than one) for writing a poem that is in some way like his poetry. There is, in the writing suggestions, along with an idea which will help you to get started with your poem and keep going with it, a good deal of emphasis on being experimental and free. It is not that there is no work involved in writing poetry. But it is a kind of work that you discover how to do while you're writing. And it seems that it can best be discovered by beginning with freedom and pleasure and ease, and by being attentive to your own inclinations and open to many different possibilities.

The usual kind of thinking, in fact, can get in the way for a beginning writer. This is because it is not mainly your intellect that you use to write poetry, but what might be called your imaginative intelligence, which is different. Writing poetry, you think more the way you do when you daydream or make a joke or talk with your friends than the way you do when you write an essay or punctuate a sentence. It is a natural kind of thinking, but since it is not often talked about or specifically required in school, it is perhaps strange to find out how valuable and important it is.

So when you use the writing suggestions in this book, don't think too much before you begin, or worry about how to begin, or wonder how to make the poem right. How you start the poem isn't likely to be crucial. There isn't a right answer when you write a poem. To create something means to make something that wasn't there before, so how can there be a right answer? Try writing down the first thing that comes into your mind and whatever else comes after that, even if it's not connected. When ideas are connected in usual ways, what is said can end up being the usual thing, which may be uninteresting. Sometimes you have to get away from the usual connections in order for new ones to appear. That is one of the things inspiration is about. Try making impossible, untrue statements or being funny, crazy, or

silly. You don't always need to make your poem go to-
gether in any regular way. You could try writing in a way
that seems very unlike you. You don't have to end your
poem with something general or abstract. And "and then
I woke up" and "but it wasn't really true" kinds of end-
ings are often boring. Be as free and particular at the end
as you are in the middle. If you want to give the poem
a title, you don't have to give it one that describes the
poem. When a baby girl is born, you don't name her
Baby Girl. You name her Jill, or some other name you
like. Give your poem a title that adds something to it. It
is often good to write even when you don't feel inspired.
Inspiration may come after you start to write, but in any
case writing and trying new things will make you a better
writer. The first person to please is yourself. It is a sign
of success if you write something you like. Or if you write
in a way that you have never written before; if you say
something you've never said, or didn't know you knew;
if you find out something; or if you've put words together
in a way that seems beautiful or new or exciting. You'll
like some poems better than others, some parts of a
poem better than other parts. After you write a few
poems, you'll probably begin to be more particular
about what you want in your poems, to want to change
words or lines or add things or leave things out. That's
fine. Revision is an interesting part of writing.

If you already write poetry, you may have the idea
that being influenced by another poet will make your
poem less your own. You may want to write always in a
style that you feel is completely yours. It is helpful, per-
haps, to know that poets have always been inspired and
influenced by other poets. It is natural when you read a
good poem to feel like writing one a little bit like it. It
is natural to learn to do things from others who do them
well. Actually, the way you write poetry now is probably
mainly the result of poems you've read, songs you've

heard, things people have said to you about poetry. It's impossible not to be influenced. Think about the way you play tennis or dance or sing. Obviously, the best people to be influenced by are people who do something really well. For writing poetry, those are good poets. It is important, particularly for young poets, to try out all kinds of ways of writing and thinking about writing. It may seem risky to give up, even temporarily, writing a kind of poem you feel successful at and to write instead something unfamiliar, but if you want to write well, it is worth it.

There may be ways the poems in this book will inspire you that have nothing to do with the writing suggestions. Of course, it's fine to follow those inspirations. In any case, if you like writing, you will want to write many poems besides the ones you write in connection with this book. What you get from these poets will probably make you better at doing that.

WRITING POETRY ON YOUR OWN

Most young writers don't write poetry as well as they could because of what they think poetry has to be like: that poetry has to have rhyme and meter, or that it has to be about something profound, or that it has to use special language; they may think, too, that everything has to be worked out in advance, and that it's important to stay on the subject they start with. The poems in this book will probably change such ideas, if you have them, as will writing poems inspired by them. There are, though, a few general things it may be helpful to know right away.

Some poetry rhymes, but most of the poetry that has been written in the world doesn't rhyme. Rhyme is just one kind of sound that poets have liked, one way of helping them write their poems. It can sometimes be inspiring, but most young poets find it too limiting, and most write better poetry without it. Meter is usually limiting too, and it is equally unnecessary.

There aren't really subjects that are more appropriate for poetry than others. You can write about anything you want—about talking on the phone, looking out the window, dreaming, anything you imagine or think, see, or hear. Certain subjects have seemed right at various times, but now, as you can see from the poems in this book, poets feel free to write about everything.

Sometimes young poets make the mistake of writing about things they think they ought to care about. Or they try to transform what they care about into something poetic—they write about "friendship" and "peace" and the "avenues of life" instead of about a certain friend, a certain day, a certain street. Making your poem general or abstract won't make your subject more worthy of poetry. It will probably overwhelm what you're really feeling and thinking, maybe even keep you from knowing what it is. The simple and particular way you talk with your friends is most likely the way you can best say what you want to, so try that way first. Using old-fashioned poetical words can falsify what you write and take you away from what you mean. The word *baby* probably means more to you than, say, the word *infant*; and *blue* may have more color and be more full of music and memories than, say, *azure*. *Infant, azure, damsel, shimmering,* and such words can also be appealing. But any word you use, you should use because it's what you mean, not because it's poetic. Part of the pleasure of writing is being free to use all words.

As for planning everything in advance, that is, for most people, not a good way to write a poem. Often poets get some of their best ideas while they're writing. They hardly ever know in advance all they're going to say. They may start with a few words that sound good to them together, maybe with a line or two, maybe just with a feeling. Then other words and other ideas come to them while they write. Planning tends to get in the way of inspiration. And so may a deliberate decision to stay on the subject you started with. Both can limit the different things that might be good in your poem. A good poem can have more than one subject.

Planning and organizing what you write can be very useful. But probably even more important for you as a beginning writer is having enough nerve and persistence to try out new ways of writing before you feel sure of them; to talk about what you care about even though you risk feeling silly; to let yourself be inspired as you go along, even though that means losing control, a little, of where the poem is going; to write not to please some audience or other but to get the poem so that it seems right to you.

You really can be completely free in your first version of a poem—you can always revise it. There is nothing in a poem that can't be changed. A poem isn't like a painting, where the change you make covers what was there before. You can always change a poem and change it back. You can revise by cutting things out, by replacing things, by changing the way you say something, by changing the lines around, by adding new lines.

Sometimes a poem seems too short, or in any case you want to add more. Sometimes you may want to change the ending. Whatever you do in revising, try to be as easy and free about it as you were in writing the poem in the first place. Keep the first version, though. You may decide later that you want to go back to it, at least partly. You can change a poem while you're writing it, right afterward, or, of course, anytime after that. Sometimes, after you write a poem and then don't think about it for a while, when you look at that poem again in a few weeks or in a month, you may have some ideas about how to make it better right away.

The best things for a young poet to do are to read a lot of poetry and to write a lot of poetry. It's very good to have some friends who also write poetry, people you can talk about poetry with and show your work to and read theirs. Some writers like to keep some sort of journal in which they write down their thoughts and feelings, maybe even their dreams. One good thing to write, in a journal or elsewhere, is what's called stream of consciousness. That means writing, say, for a half hour or even an hour whatever comes into your head, without stopping. Don't try to make sense, and forget about spelling, punctuation, complete sentences, and everything like that. You could start by thinking about something in the past—your old room, a former friend, a park you played in. You could also try writing to music. Turn on some music (preferably without words) and write whatever the music makes you think of or see. Anything that gets you involved with writing in new ways is good: collaborating on a poem with a friend, for example—you write the first line, he writes the next, and so on. You can make rules, such as that each line has to have a color in it and the name of a city. If you know another language, even a little, do some translations. If you find any kind or form of poetry that appeals to you, try writing it yourself.

Young poets tend to worry about whether or not they're working in the right way. It is probably helpful to know that different poets work in very different ways. Some have fixed schedules; some have erratic ones. Some write easily and write a lot; for others it is harder. Some poets are always beginning new poems; others work very hard revising old poems. It is possible to write, in a short period, a good many poems you like very much. But maybe, suddenly, you will not write anything you really like for a long time. And then, just as unpredictably, you will start writing well again. It is good to be ambitious, to want to write very good poetry, to keep trying new ways of doing it. After you write for a while, you'll find the way of working that is best for you.

Walt Whitman
(1819–1892)

From "Song of Myself"

1

I celebrate myself,
And what I assume you shall assume,
For every atom belonging to me as good belongs to you.

I loafe and invite my soul,
I lean and loafe at my ease . . . . observing a spear of
   summer grass.

. . .

10

Alone far in the wilds and mountains I hunt,
Wandering amazed at my own lightness and glee,
In the late afternoon choosing a safe spot to pass the
   night,
Kindling a fire and broiling the freshkilld game,
Soundly falling asleep on the gathered leaves, my dog
   and gun by my side.

The Yankee clipper is under her three skysails . . . . she
   cuts the sparkle and scud,

My eyes settle the land . . . . I bend at her prow or shout
joyously from the deck.

The boatmen and clamdiggers arose early and stopped
for me,
I tucked my trowser-ends in my boots and went and had
a good time,
You should have been with us that day round the chow-
der-kettle.

I saw the marriage of the trapper in the open air in the
far-west . . . . the bride was a red girl,
Her father and his friends sat near by crosslegged and
dumbly smoking . . . . they had moccasins to their
feet and large thick blankets hanging from their
shoulders;
On a bank lounged the trapper . . . . he was dressed
mostly in skins . . . . his luxuriant beard and curls
protected his neck,
One hand rested on his rifle . . . . the other hand held
firmly the wrist of the red girl,
She had long eyelashes . . . . her head was bare . . . . her
coarse straight locks descended upon her voluptu-
ous limbs and reached to her feet.

The runaway slave came to my house and stopped out-
side,
I heard his motions crackling the twigs of the woodpile,
Through the swung half-door of the kitchen I saw him
limpsey and weak,
And went where he sat on a log, and led him in and
assured him,
And brought water and filled a tub for his sweated body
and bruised feet,
And gave him a room that entered from my own, and
gave him some coarse clean clothes,

And remembered perfectly well his revolving eyes and
  his awkwardness,
And remember putting plasters on the galls of his neck
  and ankles;
He staid with me a week before he was recuperated and
  passed north,
I had him sit next me at table . . . . my firelock leaned in
  the corner.

· · ·

21

I am the poet of the body
And I am the poet of the soul.

The pleasures of heaven are with me, and the pains of
  hell are with me,
The first I graft and increase upon myself . . . . the latter
  I translate into a new tongue.

I am the poet of the woman the same as the man,
And I say it is as great to be a woman as to be a man,
And I say there is nothing greater than the mother of
  men.

I chant a new chant of dilation or pride,
We have had ducking and deprecating about enough,
I show that size is only development.

Have you outstript the rest? Are you the President?
It is a trifle . . . . they will more than arrive there every
  one, and still pass on.

I am he that walks with the tender and growing night;
I call to the earth and sea half-held by the night.

Press close barebosomed night! Press close magnetic
    nourishing night!
Night of south winds! Night of the large few stars!
Still nodding night! Mad naked summer night!
Smile O voluptuous coolbreathed earth!
Earth of the slumbering and liquid trees!
Earth of departed sunset! Earth of the mountains misty-
    topt!
Earth of the vitreous pour of the full moon just tinged
    with blue!
Earth of shine and dark mottling the tide of the river!
Earth of the limpid gray of clouds brighter and clearer
    for my sake!
Far-swooping elbowed earth! Rich apple-blossomed
    earth!
Smile, for your lover comes!

Prodigal! you have given me love! .... therefore I to you
    give love!
O unspeakable passionate love!

    . . .

26
I think I will do nothing for a long time but listen,
And accrue what I hear into myself .... and let sounds
    contribute toward me.

I hear bravuras of birds .... the bustle of growing wheat
    .... gossip of flames .... clack of sticks cooking my
    meals,

I hear the sound of the human voice .... a sound I love,
I hear all sounds as they are tuned to their uses ....
    sounds of the city and sounds out of the city ....
    sounds of the day and night;

Talkative young ones to those that like them . . . . the
    recitative of fish-pedlars and fruit-pedlars . . . . the
    loud laugh of workpeople at their meals,
The angry base of disjointed friendship . . . . the faint
    tones of the sick,
The judge with hands tight to the desk, his shaky lips
    pronouncing a death-sentence,
The heave'e'yo of stevedores unlading ships by the
    wharves . . . . the refrain of the anchor-lifters;
The ring of alarm-bells . . . . the cry of fire . . . . the whirr
    of swift-streaking engines and hose-carts with
    premonitory tinkles and coloured lights,
The steam whistle . . . . the solid roll of the train of
    approaching cars;
The slow-march played at night at the head of the associ-
    ation,
They go to guard some corpse . . . . the flag-tops are
    draped with black muslin.

I hear the violoncello or man's heart complaint,
And hear the keyed cornet or else the echo of sunset.

I hear the chorus . . . . it is a grand-opera . . . . this indeed
    is music!

        . . .

33
Swift wind! Space! My soul! Now I know it is true what
    I guessed at;
What I guessed when I loafed on the grass,
What I guessed while I lay alone in my bed . . . . and again
    as I walked the beach under the paling stars of the
    morning.

My ties and ballasts leave me . . . . I travel . . . . I sail
    . . . . my elbows rest in the sea-gaps,

I skirt the sierras . . . . my palms cover continents,
I am afoot with my vision.

By the city's quadrangular houses . . . . in log-huts, or
    camping with lumbermen,
Along the ruts of the turnpike . . . . along the dry gulch
    and rivulet bed,
Hoeing my onion-patch, and rows of carrots and pars-
    nips . . . . crossing savannas . . . . trailing in forests,
Prospecting . . . . gold-digging . . . . girdling the trees of
    a new purchase,
Scorched ankle-deep by the hot sand . . . . hauling my
    boat down the shallow river;
Where the panther walks to and fro on a limb overhead
    . . . . where the buck turns furiously at the hunter,
Where the rattlesnake suns his flabby length on a rock
    . . . . where the otter is feeding on fish,
Where the alligator in his tough pimples sleeps by the
    bayou,
Where the black bear is searching for roots or honey
    . . . . where the beaver pats the mud with his paddle-
    tail;
Over the growing sugar . . . . over the cottonplant
    . . . . over the rice in its low moist field;
Over the sharp-peaked farmhouse with its scalloped
    scum and slender shoots from the gutters;
Over the western persimmon . . . . over the longleaved
    corn and the delicate blue-flowered flax;
Over the white and brown buckwheat, a hummer and a
    buzzer there with the rest,
Over the dusky green of the rye as it ripples and shades
    in the breeze;
Scaling mountains . . . . pulling myself cautiously up
    . . . . holding on by low scragged limbs,
Walking the path worn in the grass and beat through the
    leaves of the brush;

Where the quail is whistling betwixt the woods and the
 wheatlot,
Where the bat flies in the July eve . . . . where the great
 goldbug drops through the dark;
Where the flails keep time on the barn floor,
Where the brook puts out of the roots of the old tree and
 flows to the meadow,
Where cattle stand and shake away flies with the tremu-
 lous shuddering of their hides,
Where the cheese-cloth hangs in the kitchen, and and-
 irons straddle the hearth-slab, and cobwebs fall in
 festoons from the rafters;
Where triphammers crash . . . . where the press is whirl-
 ing its cylinders;
Wherever the human heart beats with terrible throes out
 of its ribs;
Where the pear-shaped balloon is floating aloft . . . .
 floating in it myself and looking composedly down;
Where the life-car is drawn on the slipnoose . . . . where
 the heat hatches pale-green eggs in the dented sand,
Where the she-whale swims with her calves and never
 forsakes them,
Where the steamship trails hindways its long pennant of
 smoke,
Where the ground-shark's fin cuts like a black ship out
 of the water,
Where the half-burned brig is riding on unknown cur-
 rents,
Where shells grow to her slimy deck, and the dead are
 corrupting below;
Where the striped and starred flag is borne at the head
 of the regiments;
Approaching Manhattan, up by the long-stretching is-
 land,
Under Niagara, the cataract falling like a veil over my
 countenance;

Upon a door-step . . . . upon the horse-block of hard
wood outside,

Upon the race-course, or enjoying pic-nics or jigs or a
good game of base-ball,

At he-festivals with blackguard gibes and ironical license
and bull-dances and drinking and laughter,

At the cider-mill, tasting the sweet of the brown sqush
. . . . sucking the juice through a straw,

At apple-peelings, wanting kisses for all the red fruit I
find,

At musters and beach-parties and friendly bees and
huskings and house-raisings;

Where the mockingbird sounds his delicious gurgles,
and cackles and screams and weeps,

Where the hay-rick stands in the barnyard, and the dry-
stalks are scattered, and the brood cow waits in the
hovel,

Where the bull advances to do his masculine work, and
the stud to the mare, and the cock is treading the
hen,

Where the heifers browse, and the geese nip their food
with short jerks;

Where the sundown shadows lengthen over the limitless
and lonesome prairie,

Where the herds of buffalo make a crawling spread of the
square miles far and near;

Where the hummingbird shimmers . . . . where the neck
of the longlived swan is curving and winding;

Where the laughing-gull scoots by the slappy shore and
laughs her near-human laugh;

Where beehives range on a gray bench in the garden
half-hid by the high weeds;

Where the band-necked partridges roost in a ring on the
ground with their heads out;

Where burial coaches enter the arched gates of a ceme-
tery;

Where winter wolves bark amid wastes of snow and ici-
cled trees;

Where the yellow-crowned heron comes to the edge of
the marsh at night and feeds upon small crabs;

Where the splash of swimmers and divers cools the warm
noon;

Where the katydid works her chromatic reed on the wal-
nut-tree over the well;

Through patches of citrons and cucumbers with silver-
wired leaves,

Through the salt-lick or orange glade . . . . or under
conical firs;

Through the gymnasium . . . . through the curtained
saloon . . . . through the office or public hall;

Pleased with the native and pleased with the foreign
. . . . pleased with the new and old,

Pleased with women, the homely as well as the hand-
some,

Pleased with the quakeress as she puts off her bonnet and
talks melodiously,

Pleased with the primitive tunes of the choir of the white-
washed church,

Pleased with the earnest words of the sweating Method-
ist preacher, or any preacher . . . . looking seriously
at the camp-meeting;

Looking in at the shop-windows in Broadway the whole
forenoon . . . . pressing the flesh of my nose to the
thick plate-glass,

Wandering the same afternoon with my face turned up
to the clouds;

My right and left arms around the sides of two friends
and I in the middle;

Coming home with the bearded and dark-cheek'd bush-
boy . . . . riding behind him at the drape of the day;

Far from the settlements studying the print of animals'
feet, or the moccasin print;

By the cot in the hospital reaching lemonade to a feverish
   patient,
By the coffined corpse when all is still, examining with a
   candle;
Voyaging to every port to dicker and adventure;
Hurrying with the modern crowd, as eager and fickle as
   any,
Hot toward one I hate, ready in my madness to knife
   him,
Solitary at midnight in my back yard, my thoughts gone
   from me a long while,
Walking the old hills of Judea with the beautiful gentle
   god by my side;
Speeding through space . . . . speeding through heaven
   and the stars,
Speeding amid the seven satellites and the broad ring
   and the diameter of eighty thousand miles,
Speeding with tailed meteors . . . . throwing fire-balls like
   the rest,
Carrying the crescent child that carries its own full
   mother in its belly:
Storming enjoying planning loving cautioning,
Backing and filling, appearing and disappearing,
I tread day and night such roads.

· · ·

I understand the large hearts of heroes,
The courage of present times and all times;
How the skipper saw the crowded and rudderless wreck
   of the steamship, and death chasing it up and down
   the storm,
How he knuckled tight and gave not back one inch, and
   was faithful of days and faithful of nights,
And chalked in large letters on a board, Be of good
   cheer, We will not desert you;
How he saved the drifting company at last,

How the lank loose-gowned women looked when boated
    from the side of their prepared graves,
How the silent old-faced infants, and the lifted sick, and
    the sharp-lipped unshaven men;
All this I swallow and it tastes good . . . . I like it well,
    and it becomes mine,
I am the man . . . . I suffered . . . . I was there.

. . .

51
The past and present wilt . . . . I have filled them and
    emptied them,
And proceed to fill my next fold of the future.

Listener up there! Here you . . . . what have you to
    confide to me?
Look in my face while I snuff the sidle of evening,
Talk honestly, for no one else hears you, and I stay only
    a minute longer.

Do I contradict myself?
Very well then . . . . I contradict myself;
I am large . . . . I contain multitudes.

I concentrate toward them that are nigh . . . . I wait on
    the door-slab.

Who has done his day's work and will soonest be through
    with his supper?
Who wishes to talk with me?

Will you speak before I am gone? Will you prove already
    too late?

. . .

52

The spotted hawk swoops by and accuses me . . . . he
  complains of my gab and my loitering.

I too am not a bit tamed . . . . I too am untranslatable,
I sound my barbaric yawp over the roofs of the world.

The last scud of day holds back for me,
It flings my likeness after the rest and true as any on the
  shadowed wilds,
It coaxes me to the vapor and the dusk.

I depart as air . . . I shake my white locks at the runaway
  sun,
I effuse my flesh in eddies and drift it in lacy jags.

I bequeath myself to the dirt to grow from the grass I
  love,
If you want me again look for me under your bootsoles.

You will hardly know who I am or what I mean,
But I shall be good health to you nevertheless,
And filter and fibre your blood.

Failing to fetch me at first keep encouraged,
Missing me one place search another,
I stop somewhere waiting for you

WALT WHITMAN

Walt Whitman wrote "Song of Myself" in 1855. The poem was inspired by an idea, by a kind of joyous vision of life. The idea was something like this: that he, Walt Whitman, and everyone else, once a part of life, were eternally connected to the rest of life; that he and everyone else were in fact life itself, and so everywhere and in everything and in everyone, seeing and hearing and feeling and understanding everything. The vision is very grand and difficult and abstract. But the poem that the vision inspired isn't difficult and abstract. That is because "Song of Myself" isn't so much an explanation of Whitman's idea as it is a celebration of it—like a celebration on the Fourth of July, for example, instead of an explanation of what it means. "Song of Myself" is a poetic celebration. It is like an exuberant inventory of the world (and so of Walt Whitman) in which he congratulates and praises all the parts of life in great detail, and all for just existing.

As is often the case in art, the idea that inspired the poem had much less influence on other poets than the way the poem was written. Walt Whitman's way of writing had a great influence on twentieth-century American poets, such as Pound, Eliot, Williams, Stevens, Frank O'Hara, as well as on poets in other countries, such as Lorca, Mayakowsky, Apollinaire. "Song of Myself" was exciting to other poets for many reasons—for its length (1,346 lines), for its confident jubilant tone, for its long loose lines written in plain language and full of unpoetic-seeming things—crocodiles and city streets and firemen and people in hospitals. And the subject was so large that anything, it seemed, could be part of it and could be included. The poem didn't unfold in a carefully poetic order. Instead, the poem was like a world where any number of things could happen at any place or any time.

Write a poem that is a song of yourself, a celebration of yourself. In ordinary life, we are constantly made aware of the limitations of our powers. In this poem forget the limitations. Write as if you actually are the way Whitman imagined that you are. Write as if you were all of life, as if you were everywhere and in all time and were everyone and everything—seeing, hearing, feeling, understanding, being everything that there is. It may help to begin your lines with the words "I am" or "I see" or "I hear" or "I know." Imagine yourself in many different places, including some you've never really been in—on a sinking ship, walking through the desert, in a burning building, at the battle of the Alamo, floating down a river. You might try, at least for part of your poem, putting a different place in every line. Say what you see and do there. Try using long lines, lines which give you space enough to describe in detail exactly who you are and what you see and hear and know. Be boastful and bold. Try making the poem very long. Let your poem keep changing its subject as it goes along, as Whitman's poem does. You will probably find, after you write it, that it all goes together in a way you wouldn't have expected.

Emily Dickinson
(1830–1886)

I HEARD A FLY BUZZ

I heard a Fly buzz—when I died—
The Stillness in the Room
Was like the Stillness in the Air—
Between the Heaves of Storm—

The Eyes around—had wrung them dry—
And Breaths were gathering firm
For that last Onset—when the King
Be witnessed—in the Room—

I willed my Keepsakes—Signed away
What portion of me be
Assignable—and then it was
There interposed a Fly—

With Blue—uncertain stumbling Buzz—
Between the light—and me—
And then the Windows failed—and then
I could not see to see—

THE WIND TOOK UP
THE NORTHERN THINGS

The Wind took up the Northern Things
And piled them in the south—
Then gave the East unto the West
And opening his mouth

The four Divisions of the Earth
Did make as to devour
While everything to corners slunk
Behind the awful power—

The Wind—unto his Chambers went
And nature ventured out—
Her subjects scattered into place
Her systems ranged about

Again the smoke from Dwellings rose
The Day abroad was heard—
How intimate, a Tempest past
The Transport of the Bird—

WE LIKE MARCH

We like March—his shoes are Purple.
He is new and high—
Makes he Mud for Dog and Peddler—
Makes he Forests Dry—
Knows the Adder's Tongue his coming

And begets her spot—
Stands the Sun so close and mighty—
That our Minds are hot.
News is he of all the others—
Bold it were to die
With the Blue Birds buccaneering
On his British sky—

BEE! I'M EXPECTING YOU!

Bee! I'm expecting you!
Was saying Yesterday
To Somebody you know
That you were due—

The Frogs got Home last Week—
Are settled, and at work—
Birds, mostly back—
The Clover warm and thick—

You'll get my Letter by
The seventeenth; Reply
Or better, be with me—
Yours, Fly.

THE LAST NIGHT THAT
SHE LIVED

The last Night that She lived
It was a Common Night
Except the Dying—this to Us
Made Nature different

We noticed smallest things—
Things overlooked before
By this great light upon our Minds
Italicized—as 'twere.

As We went out and in
Between Her final Room
And Rooms where Those to be alive
Tomorrow were, a Blame

That Others could exist
While She must finish quite
A Jealousy for Her arose
So nearly infinite—

We waited while She passed—
It was a narrow time—
Too jostled were Our Souls to speak
At length the notice came.

She mentioned, and forgot—
Then lightly as a Reed
Bent to the Water, struggled scarce—
Consented, and was dead—

And We—We placed the Hair—
And drew the Head erect—

And then an awful leisure was
Belief to regulate—

THE CRICKETS SANG

The Crickets sang
And set the Sun
And Workmen finished one by one
Their Seam the Day upon.

The low Grass loaded with the Dew
The Twilight stood, as Strangers do
With Hat in Hand, polite and new
To stay as if, or go.

A Vastness, as a Neighbor, came,
A Wisdom, without Face, or Name
A Peace, as Hemispheres at Home
And so the Night became.

BECAUSE I COULD NOT STOP FOR DEATH

Because I could not stop for Death—
He kindly stopped for me—
The Carriage held but just Ourselves—
And Immortality.

We slowly drove—He knew no haste
And I had put away
My labor and my leisure too,
For His Civility—

We passed the School, where Children strove
At Recess—in the Ring—
We passed the Fields of Gazing Grain—
We passed the Setting Sun—

Or rather—He passed Us—
The Dews drew quivering and chill—
For only Gossamer, my Gown—
My Tippet—only Tulle—

We paused before a House that seemed
A Swelling of the Ground—
The Roof was scarcely visible—
The Cornice—in the Ground—

Since then—'tis Centuries—and yet
Feels shorter than the Day
I first surmised the Horses' Heads
Were toward Eternity—

EMILY DICKINSON

Emily Dickinson, born in 1830 in Amherst, Massachusetts, lived a very secluded life. She was alone most of the time; she didn't know other writers. Almost no one knew she wrote poetry. She wrote her poems in the midst of doing other things. She wrote them on the backs of envelopes and on other scraps of paper. These poems were discovered, and published, only after her death. These circumstances probably have something to do with the peculiar way her poetry is written, the way it's unlike anyone else's—with its odd use of capitals, dashes, and strange rhymes—and with its peculiar point of view. She seems to have been, more than other poets, writing just for herself.

Her way of looking at things seems, at first, innocent, like the innocence of children. But Emily Dickinson knows and feels things that children don't. Her view is not so much innocent, really, as it is gentle and resigned to the way things are. It's as if she felt that simply watching were the only thing left to do. She watches nature—trees, brooks, bees, flies, flowers, snakes, wind. She watches people. She seems even to watch herself in the same way she watches everything else—with impartial curiosity and from a distance.

In Emily Dickinson's poetry, the whole universe becomes very private and domestic. It is as if all of nature, all its gentle and violent forces, were noticed and wondered about with the kind of simple familiarity with which you might wonder about your neighbors. And everything that happens seems almost equally important. The arrival of winter, a storm, or the coming of death gets no more space than a bird's song or a fly's buzz. This makes her poems about death seem particularly strange and chilling. Emily Dickinson seems to have become as used to death as others get used to other supposedly grand and awesome things, like the Pacific Ocean, or the midnight sun, or the Alps.

So, reading her poems, you may feel a bit dizzy, as if the balance of things had been changed. That balance has to do with one's feelings. The closer something is to you, the more your own feelings are involved, the more difficult it is to be objective. It is almost impossible for most people, for instance, to consider their own deaths in a simple and objective way, as Emily Dickinson seems to in her poems. She dies and a fly buzzes—and she watches and writes.

Write a poem that is written in somewhat the same way as "I Heard a Fly Buzz"; that is, write about something that is terribly significant to you—the end of the world, the beginning of the world, your death, your birth—and in the same poem write about something that is very insignificant—a leaf dropping, the sound of a footstep, the telephone ringing, combing your hair. Don't say what your emotions are, and don't try to make an obvious connection between what is important and what isn't. Let them simply be happening at the same time: "I heard something drop when the world began." It may help if you think of it all as having happened a long time ago—if you're thinking of another century, you can probably calmly and objectively imagine both a rose blooming and a volcano erupting. Great distances of time and space make everything begin to even out.

Try using very short lines and very simple words. Use dashes and extra capital letters if they seem inspiring.

Gerard Manley Hopkins
(1844–1889)

PIED BEAUTY

Glory be to God for dappled things—
    For skies of couple-colour as a brinded cow;
        For rose-moles all in stipple upon trout that
           swim;
Fresh-firecoal chestnut-falls; finches' wings;
    Landscape plotted and pierced—fold, fallow, and
      plough;
        And áll trádes, their gear and tackle and trim.

All things counter, original, spare, strange;
    Whatever is fickle, freckled (who knows how?)
        With swift, slow; sweet, sour; adazzle, dim;
He fathers-forth whose beauty is past change:
        Praise him.

HEAVEN-HAVEN
A nun takes the veil

I have desired to go
    Where springs not fail,
To fields where flies no sharp and sided hail
    And a few lilies blow.

And I have asked to be
    Where no storms come,
Where the green swell is in the heavens dumb,
    And out of the swing of the sea.

GOD'S GRANDEUR

The world is charged with the grandeur of God.
    It will flame out, like shining from shook foil;
    It gathers to a greatness, like the ooze of oil
Crushed. Why do men then now not reck his rod?
Generations have trod, have trod, have trod;
    And all is seared with trade; bleared, smeared with
      toil;
    And wears man's smudge and shares man's smell:
      the soil
Is bare now, nor can foot feel, being shod.

And for all this, nature is never spent;
    There lives the dearest freshness deep down things;
And though the last lights off the black West went
    Oh, morning, at the brown brink eastward,
      springs—

Because the Holy Ghost over the bent
World broods with warm breast and with ah! bright
   wings.

FELIX RANDAL

Felix Randal the farrier, O is he dead then? my duty all
   ended,
Who have watched his mould of man, big-boned and
   hardy-handsome
Pining, pining, till time when reason rambled in it and
   some
Fatal four disorders, fleshed there, all contended?

Sickness broke him. Impatient he cursed at first, but
   mended
Being anointed and all; though a heavenlier heart began
   some
Months earlier, since I had our sweet reprieve and ran-
   som
Tendered to him. Ah well, God rest him all road ever he
   offended!

This seeing the sick endears them to us, us too it en-
   dears.
My tongue had taught thee comfort, touch had quenched
   thy tears,
Thy tears that touched my heart, child, Felix, poor Felix
   Randal;

How far from then forethought of, all thy more boister-
   ous years,

When thou at the random grim forge, powerful amidst
    peers,
Didst fettle for the great grey drayhorse his bright and
    battering sandal!

SPRING AND FALL:
To a young child

Márgarét, áre you gríeving
Over Goldengrove unleaving?
Leáves líke the things of man, you
With your fresh thoughts care for, can you?
Áh! ás the heart grows older
It will come to such sights colder
By and by, nor spare a sigh
Though worlds of wanwood leafmeal lie;
And yet you wíll weep and know why.
Now no matter, child, the name:
Sórrow's spríngs áre the same.
Nor mouth had, no nor mind, expressed
What heart heard of, ghost guessed:
It ís the blight man was born for,
It is Margaret you mourn for.

THE LEADEN ECHO
AND THE GOLDEN ECHO
(Maiden's song from St. Winefred's Well)

THE LEADEN ECHO

How to kéep—is there ány any, is there none such, no-
    where known some, bow or brooch or braid or
    brace, láce, latch or catch or key to keep
Back beauty, keep it, beauty, beauty, beauty, . . . from
    vanishing away?
Ó is there no frowning of these wrinkles, rankèd wrinkles
    deep,
Dówn? no waving off of these most mournful messen-
    gers, still messengers, sad and stealing messengers
    of grey?
No there's none, there's none, O no there's none,
Nor can you long be, what you now are, called fair,
Do what you may do, what, do what you may,
And wisdom is early to despair.
Be beginning; since, no, nothing can be done
To keep at bay
Age and age's evils, hoar hair,
Ruck and wrinkle, drooping, dying, death's worst, wind-
    ing sheets, tombs and worms and tumbling to decay;
So be beginning, be beginning to despair.
O there's none; no no no there's none:
Be beginning to despair, to despair,
Despair, despair, despair, despair.

THE GOLDEN ECHO

    Spare!
There is one, yes I have one (Hush there!);
Only not within seeing of the sun,
Not within the singeing of the strong sun,
Tall sun's tingeing, or treacherous the tainting of the
    earth's air,
Somewhere elsewhere there is ah well where! one,
Óne. Yes I cán tell such a key, I dó know such a place,
Where whatever's prized and passes of us, everything
    that's fresh and fast flying of us, seems to us sweet
    of us and swiftly away with, done away with, undone,
Undone, done with, soon done with, and yet dearly and
    dangerously sweet
Of us, the wimpled-water-dimpled, not-by-morning-
    matchèd face,
The flower of beauty, fleece of beauty, too too apt to, ah!
    to fleet,
Never fleets móre, fastened with the tenderest truth
To its own best being and its loveliness of youth: it is an
    everlastingness of, O it is an all youth!
Come then, your ways and airs and looks, locks, maiden
    gear, gallantry and gaiety and grace,
Winning ways, airs innocent, maiden manners, sweet
    looks, loose locks, long locks, lovelocks, gaygear,
    going gallant, girlgrace—
Resign them, sign them, seal them, send them, motion
    them with breath,
And with sighs soaring, soaring síghs deliver
Them; beauty-in-the-ghost, deliver it, early now, long
    before death
Give beauty back, beauty, beauty, beauty, back to God,
    beauty's self and beauty's giver.

See; not a hair is, not an eyelash, not the least lash lost; every hair
Is, hair of the head, numbered.
Nay, what we had lighthanded left in surly the mere mould
Will have waked and have waxed and have walked with the wind what while we slept,
This side, that side hurling a heavyheaded hundredfold
What while we, while we slumbered.
O then, weary then whý should we tread? O why are we so haggard at the heart, so care-coiled, care-killed, so fagged, so fashed, so cogged, so cumbered,
When the thing we freely fórfeit is kept with fonder a care,
Fonder a care kept than we could have kept it, kept
Far with fonder a care (and we, we should have lost it) finer, fonder
A care kept.—Where kept? Do but tell us where kept, where.—
Yonder.—What high as that! We follow, now we follow.—
Yonder, yes yonder, yonder,
Yonder.

GERARD MANLEY HOPKINS

Gerard Manley Hopkins was a Jesuit priest. His belief in God was at the center of his life. Nature and poetry were also immensely important to him, but his love of both of these was very much connected to his feelings about God. The constantly changing beauty of nature was for him a demonstration of God's power and splendor and kindness to mankind. And poetry was a way of responding to and appreciating the greatness of God as it was seen in nature, and it was also a way of communicating this grandeur and beauty to others. The poem was as much a product of God's grace and grandeur as the peach tree.

Hopkins's poems are a mixture of description, excitement, and praise. If Hopkins looked at the sunrise, it excited him not only because it was beautiful, but because in its beauty he saw God and God's generosity. Each moving moment in nature, then, was like a religious vision. Still, the things he sees in these visions don't become misty and vague and spiritual. It's in the real physical way that things are, in the exact details of that particular tree or field or sunset or cloud, that Hopkins finds God. In fact, as Hopkins shows in his poems and writes in his letters and journal, the more peculiar and particular something is, the more it suggests to him God's perfection. This feeling makes his poems unlike a great many poems about nature, religious or not, which tend to find beauty most in changelessness, permanence, and symmetry—vast oceans, lofty blue skies, snow-capped mountains—and tend to generalize and make things more like idealized pictures than like the exact way things are when you are really there. When you look closely, you see that nature is never really still and finished but is always changing and new, full of sap and juice, blowing and bending and blossoming and shining and agitating, within infinite combinations of light and weather. All this activity makes each thing slightly (or maybe greatly) different each time you see it. Hopkins seems to admire things most when they are most momentary, most energetically particular—bent, gnarled, twisted branches; "leafmeal" cloud fragments scudding across the sky; the shining reflection of light from a shaken fencing foil. His poems are not calm, objective descriptions of what he sees but an intense mingling of what he sees—that is, the way it looks in that instant—with the excitement he feels in seeing it.

Hopkins uses peculiar, eccentric words in his poems, dialect words, archaic words, and words that he makes up, usually combinations of already existing words, such as *leafmeal*, *fresh-firecoal*, *chestnut-falls*. The word combinations put the movement and the moment and the thing together (*wimpled-water-dimpled*) so that sometimes it's a combination which is so particular that it seems made to be used only once—for that particular instance. It's as if he wants the poems to contain those very clouds or trees or birds; and for the poem to be as full of change and life as they are. His poems do in fact seem almost a physical experience. It is almost impossible to read one in a calm, quiet way. The poems—with their crowded lines that sometimes seem bursting with too many words, with their speed-ups and slowdowns and unexpected stops, with their alliteration and internal rhymes—turn out to be as odd and individual as the things and moments in nature that inspired them. You become, in reading the poems, a little breathless. In the midst of a description, Hopkins connects what he's seeing and feeling with God, whom he feels to be the cause of it. And sometimes he stops to exclaim over the amazingness of it all: "and with ah! bright wings."

"Pied Beauty" is a poem of praise to God for creating all the odd things that Hopkins finds such beauty in. It is a list of such things, with praise at the beginning and at the end. Lines 2–5 list things in nature: a sky he saw, a trout, a chestnut tree, finches' wings, farmed and divided-up landscapes. Line 6 praises the tools and gear of trades like carpentry and blacksmithing. The second stanza is in general praise of oddness everywhere. The form of this poem is as eccentric as the things it praises. Hopkins called it a "curtal" (curtailed or shortened) sonnet. Instead of being 14 lines divided into parts of 8 lines and 6 lines, it is 10 and a fraction lines, divided into stanzas of 6 lines and a little over 4 lines. It is full of strange words: *couple-colour*, a made-up combined word suggesting two-colored, with the colors right together, a couple; *brinded*, an old, no longer used form of the word *brindled*, which means streaked or spotted with a darker color; *rose-moles*, a made-up combined word which describes the look of spots on trout. *Fresh-firecoal chestnut-falls* is a four-word combination that suggests chestnuts in autumn falling or fallen to the ground in the way that coals fall in a grate while the fire burns—it is impossible to be sure exactly what it means, but it probably is something like that. Hopkins's descriptions are often like this —like the first excited glimpse of something, perhaps while it's moving and before you know exactly what it is you're seeing.

Write a poem in which you say how much you like a whole lot of different things of a particular kind. You could praise round things, whatever's blue or orange or purple, sparkling things, flat things, things that are triangular or heavy or new. Begin with one thing—say, an icy window if you're writing about cold things or square things or white ones—and then just go on naming others as you think of them. When you mention each thing, think of some particular time you've seen it, and try to get the way it looked at that time into what you say. One way to do that is to make up a word combination—a combination of words that is so particular, that gets the color and shape and movement of things so exactly, that it could perhaps be used only once, only to describe what you see at that one second in your life—"skies of couple-colour as a brinded cow." You can try alliteration, too, if you like, and rhymes that are inside of lines.

Arthur Rimbaud
(1854–1891)

Three poems from The Illuminations

AFTER THE FLOOD

As soon as the idea of the Flood had subsided, a hare paused among the sainfoins and the swaying bellflowers, and said his prayer to the rainbow through the spider's web.

Oh! the precious stones that were hiding,—the flowers that already looked around.

In the filthy main street butchers' stalls rose, and barges were tugged toward the sea rising up in tiers as in engravings.

Blood flowed, at Bluebeard's,—in slaughterhouses, —in circuses, where the seal of God whitened the windows. Blood and milk flowed.

Beavers did their building. Glasses of black coffee steamed in the cafés.

In the still dripping big house with glass panes, children in mourning looked at the marvelous reflections.

A door slammed, and, in the village square, the child waved his arms, understood by weather vanes and cocks on steeples everywhere, under the glittering downpour.

Madame * * * installed a piano in the Alps. Mass and first communions were celebrated at the hundred thousand altars of the cathedral.

Caravans departed. And the Hotel Splendide was erected in the chaos of ice and of polar night.

From that time, the Moon heard jackals howling through the wildernesses of thyme—and eclogues in wooden shoes grumbling in the orchard. Then, in the forest, violet-hued, burgeoning, Eucharis told me that it was spring.

Gush forth, pond;—Foam, roll above the bridge and over the woods;—black palls and organs,—lightning and thunder,—rise up and roll;—Waters and sorrows, rise up and release the Floods again.

For since they have vanished,—oh! the precious stones burying themselves, and the opened flowers!—it's a nuisance! and the Queen, the Sorceress who kindles her coals in the earthen pot, will never be willing to tell us what she knows, and what we do not know.

DAWN

I embraced the summer dawn.

Nothing was stirring yet in front of the palaces. The water lay lifeless. Encamped shadows did not leave the woodland road. I stepped forth, arousing breaths alive and warm, and precious stones kept watch, and wings rose up without a sound.

My first enterprise was, in the path already filled with cool, pale glints, a flower that told me her name.

I laughed at the blond waterfall which tossed disheveled hair across the pines: on the silvery summit I espied the goddess.

Then, one by one, I lifted her veils. In the lane, waving my arms. On the plain, where I gave the cock notice of her coming. In the city, she fled among the steeples and domes, and, running like a beggar across the marble quays, I pursued her.

On the upper part of the road, near a grove of laurels, I surrounded her with her massed veils, and I sensed somewhat her immeasurable body. Dawn and the child plunged to the bottom of the wood.

When I awoke, it was noon.

ROYALTY

One fine morning, in the country of a very gentle people, a superb man and woman were crying out in the public square: "My friends, I want her to be queen!" "I want to be queen!" She laughed and trembled. He spoke to friends of revelation, of a trial terminated. They swooned against each other.

In fact, they were monarchs for an entire morning, during which crimson hangings were raised again on the houses, and for the entire afternoon, during which they moved forward toward the gardens of palm trees.

translated by Enid Rhodes Peschel

THE LICE SEEKERS

When the child's forehead full of red torments
Begs for the white swarm of indistinct dreams
There come close to his bed two big charming sisters
With frail fingers and silver nails.

They seat the child next to a window
Wide open, where blue air bathes a confusion of flowers
And in his heavy hair where the dew falls
Promenade their delicate fingers, terrible and enchant-
    ing.

He hears the singing of their timorous breath
Which bears the scent of long vegetable and rosy honeys
And which a whistling interrupts now and then, salivas
Taken back from the lip or desires for kisses.

He hears their black eyelashes beating beneath per-
    fumed
Silences; and their fingers electric and sweet
Make crackle among his hazy indolences
Beneath their royal fingernails the death of little lice.

Now there is mounting in him the wine of Laziness,
Harmonica's sigh which could be delirious;
The child feels, according to the slowness of the ca-
    resses,
Spring up and die unceasingly a wish to cry.

translated by Kenneth Koch and Georges Guy

POETS SEVEN YEARS OLD

And the mother, closing the exercise book,
Went off satisfied and very proud, not seeing
In the blue eyes and beneath the bumpy forehead
That her child's soul was filled with revulsions.

All day he sweated obedience; very
Intelligent; but certain nasty habits, several traits,
Seemed to show bitter hypocrisies in him.
Passing through dark halls with musty drapes
He would stick out his tongue, his two fists
In his groin, and in his closed eyes see dots.
A door would be open to evening; by lamplight
He could be seen upstairs sulking on the banister
Beneath a gulf of day which hung from the roof. In
    summer
Above all, vanquished, stupid, he would stubbornly
Lock himself up in the coolness of latrines.
He would think there, tranquil, dilating his nostrils.

When in winter the little garden behind the house,
Washed of the smells of the day, became immooned,
He, stretched out at the foot of a wall, buried in the mud
And pressing his eye flat so as to have visions,
Would listen to the swarming of the scaly trellises.
As for pity! his only intimates were those children—
Feeble, with blank foreheads, eyes fading on their
    cheeks,
Hiding thin fingers yellow and black with mud
Under clothes stinking of diarrhea and all shabby—
Who conversed with the gentleness of idiots;
And if having discovered him at such filthy pities
His mother became frightened, the deep tenderness

Of the child would overwhelm her surprise.
It was good. She would have the blue look—that lies!

At seven he was writing novels about life
In the great desert where ecstatic Liberty shines,
Forests, suns, banks, savannas! He was aided
By illustrated papers in which, blushing, he looked
At Spanish and Italian women laughing.
When, brown-eyed, mad, in printed cotton dresses
—Aged eight—the daughter of the workers next door
Had come, the little brute, and when she had jumped
On his back in a corner, shaking her braids,
And he was underneath her, he would bite her buttocks
(For she never wore panties)
And then bruised by her fists and by her heels
He would take the savors of her skin back to his room.

He dreaded the pale Sundays of December
When, all spruced up, at a little round mahogany table
He would read a Bible edged in cabbage-green.
Dreams oppressed him each night in the alcove.
He loved not God, but the men whom in the russet
     evening,
Dark, in blouses, he would see returning to the suburbs
Where the criers with three rollings of the drum
Make the crowds laugh and groan at proclamations.
He dreamed of the amorous meadow, where luminous
Billows, healthy perfumes, golden pubescences
Make their calm movement and take their flight;

And how he savoured, most of all, somber things,
When, in the bare room with closed shutters,
High and blue, filled with an acrid dampness,
He would read his novel, which he always thought about,
Full of heavy clayey skies and drowned forests,

Of flesh-flowers opened in the depths of celestial
    woods—
Dizziness, failings, routs, and pity!—
While the din of the neighborhood sounded
Below, alone, lying on pieces of unbleached
Canvas, with a violent premonition of sails! . . .

    translated by Kenneth Koch and Georges Guy

VOWELS

Black A, white E, red I, green U, blue O—vowels,
I'll tell, some day, your secret origins:
A, black hairy corset of dazzling flies
Who boom around cruel stenches,

Gulfs of darkness; E, candor of steam and of tents,
Lances of proud glaciers, white kings, Queen-Anne's-
    lace shivers;
I, deep reds, spit blood, laughter of beautiful lips
In anger or in drunkenness and penitence;

U, cycles, divine vibrations of dark green oceans,
Peacefulness of pastures dotted with animals, the peace
    of wrinkles
Which alchemy prints on studious foreheads;

O, supreme trumpet, full of strange harsh sounds,
Silences which are crossed by Worlds and by Angels—
    O, Omega, violet ray of Her Eyes!

    translated by Kenneth Koch

ARTHUR RIMBAUD

Arthur Rimbaud wrote all his poems between the ages of fifteen and twenty. After that, he stopped writing—no one is sure why. No other poet has written so much amazing poetry at such a young age.

Rimbaud thought that poetry had a power that nothing else had, because poetry could be a way to see beyond reality. He thought that what people called reality was only a surface, and beyond that surface a lot more was going on. Usually people only saw the surface, but if a visionary poet were in a certain inspired state of mind, he could find the words to describe this other life that was there but that most people could never see. Rimbaud at one time believed that he could even find another language, made up not just of words but also of colors and tastes and textures and fragrances. His sonnet "Vowels" is a reference to that language.

"After the Flood," "Dawn," and "Royalty" are from a series of poems called *The Illuminations.* In each one of the poems, his vision of something is illuminated or lighted up. Almost all the poems in *The Illuminations* are written not in verse but in what is called prose poetry, poetry which is not divided into lines and which doesn't have rhyme and meter. Prose poetry is one of the forms of poetry.

Often, the poems in *The Illuminations* seem to be about some particular moment which is so brief or vague or complicated that it would ordinarily be hard to talk about or even to see. "After the Flood," for instance, is a vision of the beautiful, strange in-between moment when the Great Flood ends and spring begins. "Dawn" is about the moment when day is just barely beginning. "Royalty" seems to base a whole story on a momentary feeling of affection between a man and a woman.

Rimbaud doesn't write about the way these moments really look. Rather, in the poems, these moments seemed to be turned into wonderful pictures or stories that show their amazingness and beauty and complexity. Think of the way a real dawn seems to be—you look, and suddenly, mysteriously, it is no longer dark, it is light. But Rimbaud's vision of the dawn in his poem dramatizes its mystery and excitement. The in-between time, when it is just getting to be light, is expanded into a whole story, in which Dawn is a seductive and beautiful and elusive goddess wrapped in endless veils of air. The boy, after chasing her, finally hugs her, and falls asleep next to her, and wakes up at noon without her.

"After the Flood" lists the things that go on after the Flood subsides, in the moment of change when some amazing first springtime is just beginning. This wonderful moment seems to be taking place everywhere. It is like a kind of world-wide holiday in which all life is involved—spiders, beavers, caravans, and flowers—and in which everything is suddenly possible. After the change is complete, boredom and sameness return, and Rimbaud wants the Flood to come back so that the world will be entirely new and strange and wonderful again. Especially since the mysterious queen who knows the secret of how it all happened will never reveal the truth about it. In Rimbaud's poem "Royalty," a village lets a man and woman celebrate their love for each other by becoming king and queen and ruling for a day.

Write a prose poem about your own vision of some wonderful in-between moment in which things change. You could write about a moment in nature—the time just before or just after a rainstorm or a snowstorm, the time just before it gets dark. Or you could write about yourself —about the moment of waking up or of going to sleep or of falling in love or of making a decision about something. But don't write about what the time is really like. Instead, turn it into a strange and beautiful picture or story. Remember that anything is possible. The vision can be taking place everywhere and in all time. Inanimate things can come alive and speak. There can be exotic mixtures of weather and landscapes. Think of what you would like to see happening—in cities, in the country, on the ocean, in houses, in schools, in beehives, in cloud banks, in the center of a flower. Remember that in visions, as in dreams, every detail means something and is important, so really try to see everything and describe it in great detail. Think of colors and tastes, fragrances, sounds, and textures—and make them all part of some beautiful and unreal place and time. You might like to make your poem, like "After the Flood," mostly a list of what is going on everywhere. Or you might like to try, as in "Royalty," writing a little story or drama. Just begin with a scene and let the beautiful details of the scene inspire the story, with one amazing thing happening after another. Don't worry about the plot. In this kind of writing, the plot is less important than the beauty of the details. You could give your poem a title—like "Dusk" or "The Great Snow"—which makes it clear what the poem is about.

A NOTE ON TRANSLATION

SENSATION

Par les soirs bleus d'été, j'irai dans les sentiers,
Picoté par les blés, fouler l'herbe menue:
Rêveur, j'en sentirai la fraîcheur à mes pieds.
Je laisserai le vent baigner ma tête nue.

Je ne parlerai pas, je ne penserai rien:
Mais l'amour infini me montera dans l'âme,
Et j'irai loin, bien loin, comme un bohémien,
Par la Nature,—heureux comme avec une femme.

SENSATION

On blue summer evenings I'll go down the pathways
Pricked by the grain, crushing the tender grass—
Dreaming, I'll feel its coolness on my feet.
I'll let the wind bathe my bare head.

I won't talk at all, I won't think about anything,
But infinite love will rise in my soul,
And I'll go far, very far, like a gypsy,
Into Nature—happy, as if with a woman.

A translation of a poem is not the same as the original, but it can be close to it. Without translation a lot of marvelous poetry would never be known to people who didn't know the language it was written in. You should know that there are good and bad translations, so don't give up on a foreign-language poet if you read a translation you don't like. That may be the translator's fault. Translating poems yourself can be very enjoyable and good for your writing and reading of poetry.

Rimbaud's poem "Sensation" is beautiful, simple, and short. Obviously, it's hard, probably impossible, to get all of its good qualities into any other language. It seems worthwhile, though, to try to get some of the grace and spontaneity and force of "Sensation" into English poetry, where there is nothing quite like it. To do so, as always in translating poetry, one has to give up some things in order to have others.

The French poem rhymes and has a regular meter, and this, combined with the casualness and ease of the way it says things, gives it a very pleasant sound. I found in translating the poem that if I tried to keep the rhyme and meter, it didn't sound natural. I gave up the rhyme and meter so that I could get, instead, the easy conversational tone.

One thing that is hard in translating is that words in different languages often don't correspond to each other exactly—you can't rely completely on a dictionary. For example, the French word *soir* means both afternoon and evening. So, in translating it into English, you have to choose one or the other. Neither word, though, gives quite the sense of long, long summer afternoons that is in the original. Also, even if words mean approximately the same thing in the two languages, the people who speak these languages may have different feelings about them. The closest English equivalent of the French word *âme* is soul. But in English, *soul* has almost entirely religious associations, whereas in French *âme* also suggests a place where strong feelings are—more like *heart* in English.

If you are beginning to translate a poem, remember that the meaning and the tone are almost always much more important in giving a sense of what the poem is like than its meter and rhyme scheme. Trying to get the rhyme and meter can lead to adding words, distorting word order and meaning, and doing other things that make the poem inaccurate and awkward. Sometimes a good translation comes quickly, but usually it goes through a number of versions.

As for reading, of course it's best to read the original poem. If you know the original language slightly, you can use a translation to help you read the original. If you're reading good translations, reading a number of poems by the same poet gives you a better chance of getting a feeling for what the original poem is like. If you like the work of the poet you're reading in translation, you may be inspired to learn his language. It was so I could read French poetry—mainly Rimbaud and Apollinaire—that I learned French.

Kenneth Koch

William Butler Yeats

(1865 – 1939)

THE SONG OF WANDERING AENGUS

I went out to the hazel wood,
Because a fire was in my head,
And cut and peeled a hazel wand,
And hooked a berry to a thread;
And when white moths were on the wing,
And moth-like stars were flickering out,
I dropped the berry in a stream
And caught a little silver trout.

When I had laid it on the floor
I went to blow the fire aflame,
But something rustled on the floor,
And someone called me by my name:
It had become a glimmering girl
With apple blossom in her hair
Who called me by my name and ran
And faded through the brightening air.

Though I am old with wandering
Through hollow lands and hilly lands,
I will find out where she has gone,

And kiss her lips and take her hands;
And walk among long dappled grass,
And pluck till time and times are done
The silver apples of the moon,
The golden apples of the sun.

HE WISHES FOR THE
CLOTHS OF HEAVEN

Had I the heavens' embroidered cloths,
Enwrought with golden and silver light,
The blue and the dim and the dark cloths
Of night and light and the half-light,
I would spread the cloths under your feet:
But I, being poor, have only my dreams;
I have spread my dreams under your feet;
Tread softly because you tread on my dreams.

ADAM'S CURSE

We sat together at one summer's end,
That beautiful mild woman, your close friend,
And you and I, and talked of poetry.
I said: 'A line will take us hours maybe;
Yet if it does not seem a moment's thought,
Our stitching and unstitching has been naught.

Better go down upon your marrow-bones
And scrub a kitchen pavement, or break stones

Like an old pauper, in all kinds of weather;
For to articulate sweet sounds together
Is to work harder than all these, and yet
Be thought an idler by the noisy set
Of bankers, schoolmasters, and clergymen
The martyrs call the world.'

                       And thereupon
That beautiful mild woman for whose sake
There's many a one shall find out all heartache
On finding that her voice is sweet and low
Replied: 'To be born woman is to know—
Although they do not talk of it at school—
That we must labour to be beautiful.'

I said: 'It's certain there is no fine thing
Since Adam's fall but needs much labouring.
There have been lovers who thought love should be
So much compounded of high courtesy
That they would sigh and quote with learned looks
Precedents out of beautiful old books;
Yet now it seems an idle trade enough.'

We sat grown quiet at the name of love;
We saw the last embers of daylight die,
And in the trembling blue-green of the sky,
A moon, worn as if it had been a shell
Washed by time's waters as they rose and fell
About the stars and broke in days and years.

I had a thought for no one's but your ears:
That you were beautiful, and that I strove
To love you in the old high way of love;
That it had all seemed happy, and yet we'd grown
As weary-hearted as that hollow moon.

THE WILD SWANS AT COOLE

The trees are in their autumn beauty,
The woodland paths are dry,
Under the October twilight the water
Mirrors a still sky;
Upon the brimming water among the stones
Are nine-and-fifty swans.

The nineteenth autumn has come upon me
Since I first made my count;
I saw, before I had well finished,
All suddenly mount
And scatter wheeling in great broken rings
Upon their clamorous wings.

I have looked upon those brilliant creatures,
And now my heart is sore.
All's changed since I, hearing at twilight,
The first time on this shore,
The bell-beat of their wings above my head,
Trod with a lighter tread.

Unwearied still, lover by lover,
They paddle in the cold
Companionable streams or climb the air;
Their hearts have not grown old;
Passion or conquest, wander where they will,
Attend upon them still.

But now they drift on the still water,
Mysterious, beautiful;
Among what rushes will they build,
By what lake's edge or pool
Delight men's eyes when I awake some day
To find they have flown away?

FOR ANNE GREGORY

'Never shall a young man,
Thrown into despair
By those great honey-coloured
Ramparts at your ear,
Love you for yourself alone
And not your yellow hair.'

'But I can get a hair-dye
And set such colour there,
Brown, or black, or carrot,
That young men in despair
May love me for myself alone
And not my yellow hair.'

'I heard an old religious man
But yesternight declare
That he had found a text to prove
That only God, my dear,
Could love you for yourself alone
And not your yellow hair.'

CRAZY JANE ON THE DAY OF JUDGMENT

'Love is all
Unsatisfied
That cannot take the whole
Body and soul';
And that is what Jane said.

'Take the sour
If you take me,
I can scoff and lour
And scold for an hour.'
'That's certainly the case,' said he.

'Naked I lay,
The grass my bed;
Naked and hidden away,
That black day';
And that is what Jane said.

'What can be shown?
What true love be?
All could be known or shown
If Time were but gone.'
'That's certainly the case,' said he.

WILLIAM BUTLER YEATS

William Butler Yeats was born in 1865. Though his po-
etry is comparatively traditional in its use of rhyme and
meter, in its subject matter, and in its romantic and he-
roic tone, Yeats, like other modern poets, was looking
for an original answer to the meaning of things rather
than expressing an already existing belief. And, like
many of them, he often wrote about the events of his
everyday life. The regular circumstances of being alive—
that time passes, for instance, and that things change,
that you have things, then lose them, that you get older,
then die, that these things happen mostly unpredictably
—these circumstances did not seem to Yeats to be plain
and ordinary. They seemed to him to be part of a great
mystery.

Yeats felt that behind the regular, rather haphazard
way things happened, there was something else going
on, there was perhaps an ultimate design, a system, in
which everything worked out and made sense. You can't
really see the great design clearly because while you are
alive you are still a part of it—in the way that you can't
see a whole city while you're still in it, walking down one
of its streets. In his attempts to understand it nonethe-
less, Yeats studied religions, he investigated mysticism
and all kinds of ideas, and he invented his own theories.
And sometimes the everyday events of his life—walking
into a schoolroom or talking with friends—seemed mo-
mentous, seemed like clues.

Sometimes in Yeats's poetry, everything is com-
pletely extraordinary—as when he makes up fairy tales
and legends. But even when he is writing about his own
life—about particular conversations, times, rooms, peo-
ple, feelings—he writes about it in such a way that it

seems to mean a great deal and to continually bring up questions about life in general.

Usually in Yeats's poetry, there is a strong form. He almost always uses rhyme and meter. And he writes in a lofty, rather noble-sounding tone. Both form and tone make what he says seem more solemn, more important, more meant-to-be.

Also, he chooses words and puts them together so that in addition to a particular meaning they suggest other meanings that seem more significant, more lasting. This way of using words is sometimes called symbolism. A symbol in a poem is usually something physical (for instance, the moon) which is used both to be itself (a particular moon on a particular night) and also to suggest other, perhaps immaterial, timeless qualities (the moon might suggest purity, for example, or continual change). Certain kinds of words seem more full of permanent meaning, seem weightier than others. *Grocery store* may work less well than *star* or *fire* if you are writing symbolically. Yeats is sometimes called a "symbolist poet" because he often wrote in this symbolical way.

Symbolism can seem much more difficult than it really is. Think of a church. It is symbolic. It is a real building that suggests by its architecture certain spiritual and eternal possibilities. That is, it is built so as to affect how you feel and think. But its beauty can move you whether or not you know what ideas and beliefs inspired it. To enjoy Yeats's poetry, you don't have to know where the symbols come from—from what dreams or myths or legends. Poetry has been inspired by all kinds of different beliefs and ideas and experiences, but they are never the same things as the poem. The poem is what is on the page, as the church is what is on the street. You won't find the secret of life in Yeats's poetry. But you are likely to feel something about what you do and don't know—something of the mysterious way our lives suggest a kind of sense that is always a little beyond us.

Yeats was inspired by fairy tales, folklore, legends, myths. These stories usually are intended to mean more than they actually say. "The Song of Wandering Aengus" is like a fairy tale. You know when you read it that it's not supposed to be only about the life of a fisherman named Aengus who loses his girl friend and can't ever quite get over it. The fantastic and impossible details let you know it's also about something else. The girl could "represent" beauty or poetic inspiration or youth or knowledge—anything that people have briefly, then lose and try to get back. But whatever it suggests to you, you will probably find the poem exciting, not only for the meaning but also for the magical and strange way it's written.

The stories Yeats made up about Crazy Jane are not gentle and childlike and familiar, like the story of Aengus. "Crazy Jane on the Day of Judgment" is one of the many Yeats poems that is in the form of a conversation or a little play. Yeats characteristically presents both sides of the argument in a dialogue, though here Crazy Jane has a lot more to say than God, who restricts himself to answering her somewhat ironically. Talking about sex and love, Jane says love has to be physical as well as spiritual (stanza 1), that in love you have to take the bad with the good (stanza 2), that a certain day of love was a strange and frightening experience for her (stanza 3), and in the last stanza she asks, What can anyone really know about love? Her statement that all could be known "if Time were but gone" is in one way "crazy" (as Jane is in one way crazy—how could time be "gone"?) and is in another way profound (as Jane is profound). The sense of it is that you can't really know a thing for sure as long as you and it are changing; and, if you exist in time, you are always changing—and so is everything living that's around you, and everything you feel. So, the only way you could know anything for sure might be if time stopped. Time's stopping is just about impossible to imagine, but it is something that is supposed to happen at the Last Judgment, which is when Crazy Jane's conversation is taking place.

To write a poem like one of these two, you might start by thinking of some characters (human or not). The characters could be invented by you or by someone else. They could be from the movies, from a fairy tale, from a comic strip or a myth. If you write a dialogue poem, you can, like Yeats, make one character great and powerful and the other rather ordinary or helpless. Your made-up person might talk to the wind or to a mountain or the sky or George Washington or Napoleon. Let the conversation be about something everybody is always wondering about—like beauty, love, friendship, death—but try making it a strange and unlikely conversation. If you like, let the characters bring in impossible and fantastic ideas— the idea that time is gone, that space is gone, that time goes backward, that all people are one person, that animals rule people, that the sun makes it dark, and so on. Remember, you don't have to understand why your characters say what they say, and you don't have to agree with them. A refrain, like the repeated lines *"And that is what Jane said"* and *"That's certainly the case,' said he,"* may be inspiring to use. You might like to include, as Yeats does, one or more of the characters' names in your title.

You could also write a fantastic fairy tale–like poem, like "The Song of Wandering Aengus." Don't think of making it mean something; rather, think of making it as mysterious as Yeats's poem is. Put in colorful and strange and impossible details. However strange your poem is, it will probably reflect your feelings and concerns in one way or another, as even your craziest dreams do.

Gertrude Stein
(1874–1946)

SUSIE ASADO

Sweet sweet sweet sweet sweet tea.
    Susie Asado.
Sweet sweet sweet sweet sweet tea.
    Susie Asado.
Susie Asado which is a told tray sure.
A lean on the shoe this means slips slips hers.
When the ancient light grey is clean it is yellow, it is a silver seller.
This is a please this is a please there are the saids to jelly. These are the wets these say the sets to leave a crown to Incy.
Incy is short for incubus.
A pot. A pot is a beginning of a rare bit of trees. Trees tremble, the old vats are in bobbles, bobbles which shade and shove and render clean, render clean must.
    Drink pups.
Drink pups drink pups lease a sash hold, see it shine and a bobolink has pins. It shows a nail.
What is a nail. A nail is unison.
Sweet sweet sweet sweet sweet tea.

LADIES' VOICES

CURTAIN RAISER

Ladies' voices give pleasure.

The acting two is easily lead. Leading is not in winter. Here the winter is sunny.

Does that surprise you.

Ladies voices together and then she came in.

Very well good night.

Very well good night.

(Mrs. Cardillac.)

That's silver.

You mean the sound.

Yes the sound.

ACT II

Honest to God Miss Williams I don't mean to say that I was older.

But you were.

Yes I was. I do not excuse myself. I feel that there is no reason for passing an archduke.

You like the word.

You know very well that they all call it their house.

As Christ was to Lazarus so was the founder of the hill to Mahon.

You really mean it.

I do.

ACT III

Yes Genevieve does not know it. What. That we are seeing Caesar.

Caesar kisses.

Kisses today.

Caesar kisses every day.

Genevieve does not know that it is only in this country that she could speak as she does.

She does speak very well doesn't she. She told them that there was not the slightest intention on the part of her countrymen to eat the fish that was not caught in their country.

In this she was mistaken.

ACT IV

What are ladies voices.
Do you mean to believe me.
Have you caught the sun.
Dear me have you caught the sun.

SCENE II

Did you say they were different. I said it made no difference.

Where does it. Yes.

Mr. Richard Sutherland. This is a name I know.

Yes.

The Hotel Victoria.

Many words spoken to me have seemed English.

Yes we do hear one another and yet what are called voices the best decision in telling of balls.

Masked balls.

Yes masked balls.

Poor Augustine.

YET DISH

I
Put a sun in Sunday, Sunday.
Eleven please ten hoop. Hoop.
Cousin coarse in coarse in soap.
Cousin coarse in soap sew up. soap.
Cousin coarse in sew up soap.

II
A lea ender stow sole lightly.
Not a bet beggar.
Nearer a true set jump hum,
A lamp lander so seen poor lip.

III
Never so round.
A is a guess and a piece.
A is a sweet cent sender.
A is a kiss slow cheese.
A is for age jet.

IV
New deck stairs.
Little in den little in dear den.

V
Polar pole.
Dust winder.
Core see.
A bale a bale o a bale.

VI
Extravagant new or noise peal extravagant.

VII

S a glass.
Roll ups.

VIII

Powder in wails, powder in sails, powder is all next to it
   is does wait sack rate all goals like chain in clear.

IX

Negligible old star.
Pour even.
It was a sad per cent.
Does on sun day.
Watch or water.
So soon a moon or a old heavy press.

X

Pearl cat or cat or pill or pour check.
New sit or little.
New sat or little not a wad yet.
Heavy toe heavy sit on head.

XI

Ex, ex, ex.
Bull it bull it bull it bull it.
Ex Ex Ex.

XII

Cousin plates pour a y shawl hood hair.
No see eat.

XIII

They are getting, bad left log lope, should a court say
   stream, not a dare long beat a soon port.

XIV

Colored will he.
Calamity.
Colored will he
Is it a soon. Is it a soon. Is it a soon. soon. Is it a soon.
   soon.

XV

Nobody's ice.
Nobody's ice to be knuckles.
Nobody's nut soon.
Nobody's seven picks.
Picks soap stacks.
Six in set on seven in seven told, to top.

XVI

A spread chin shone.
A set spread chin shone.

XVII

No people so sat.
Not an eider.
Not either. Not either either.

XVIII

Neglect, neglect use such.
Use such a man.
Neglect use such a man.
Such some here.

XIX

Note tie a stem bone single pair so itching.

XX

Little lane in lay in a circular crest.

X X I

peace while peace while toast.
paper eight paper eight or, paper eight ore white.

X X I I

Coop pour.
Never a single ham.
Charlie. Charlie.

X X I I I

Neglect or.
A be wade.
Earnest care lease.
Least ball sup.

X X I V

Meal dread.
Meal dread so or.
Meal dread so or bounce.
Meal dread so or bounce two sales. Meal dread so or
    bounce two sails. Not a rice. No nor a pray seat, not
    a little muscle, not a nor noble, not a cool right more
    than a song in every period of nails and pieces pieces
    places of places.

X X V

Neat know.
Play in horizontal pet soap.

X X V I

Nice pose.
Supper bell.
Pull a rope pressed.
Color glass.

XXVII

Nice oil pail.
No gold go at.
Nice oil pail.
Near a paper lag sought.
What is an astonishing won door. A please spoon.

XXVIII

Nice knee nick ear.
Not a well pair in day.
Nice knee neck core.
What is a skin pour in day.

XXIX

Climb climb max.
Hundred in wait.
Paper cat or deliver.

XXX

Little drawers of center.
Neighbor of dot light.
Shorter place to make a boom set.
Marches to be bright.

XXXI

Suppose a do sat.
Suppose a negligence.
Suppose a cold character.

XXXII

Suppose a negligence.
Suppose a sell.
Suppose a neck tie.

XXXIII

Suppose a cloth cape.
Suppose letter suppose let a paper.
Suppose soon.

XXXIV

A prim a prim prize.
A sea pin.
A prim a prim prize
A sea pin.

XXXV

Witness a way go.
Witness a way go. Witness a way go. Wetness.
Wetness.

XXXVI

Lessons lettuce.
Let us peer let us polite let us pour, let us polite. Let us
    polite.

XXXVII

Neither is blessings bean.

XXXVIII

Dew Dew Drops.
Leaves kindly Lasts.
Dew Dew Drops.

XXXIX

A R. nuisance.
Not a regular plate.
Are, not a regular plate.

XL

Lock out sandy.
Lock out sandy boot trees.

Lock out sandy boot trees knit glass.
Lock out sandy boot trees knit glass.

XLI
A R not new since.
New since.
Are new since bows less.

XLII
A jell cake.
A jelly cake.
A jelly cake.

XLIII
Peace say ray comb pomp
Peace say ray comb pump
Peace say ray comb pomp
Peace say ray comb pomp.

XLIV
Lean over not a coat low.
Lean over not a coat low by stand.
Lean over net. Lean over net a coat low hour stemmed
Lean over a coat low a great send. Lean over coat low
extra extend.

XLV
Copying Copying it in.

XLVI
Never second scent never second scent in stand. Never
second
scent in stand box or show. Or show me sales. Or show
me
sales oak. Oak pet. Oak pet stall.

XLVII

Not a mixed stick or not a mixed stick or glass. Not a
mend stone bender, not a mend stone bender or
stain.

XLVIII

Polish polish is it a hand, polish is it a hand or all, or all
poles sick, or all poles sick.

XLIX

Rush in rush in slice.

L

Little gem in little gem in an. Extra.

LI

In the between egg in, in the between egg or on.

LII

Leaves of gas, leaves of get a towel louder.

LIII

Not stretch.

LIV

Tea Fulls.
Pit it pit it little saddle pear say.

LV

Let me see wheat air blossom.
Let me see tea.

LVI

Nestle in glass, nestle in walk, nestle in fur a lining.

LVII

Pale eaten best seek.
Pale eaten best seek, neither has met is a glance.

LVIII

Suppose it is a s. Suppose it is a seal. Suppose it is a
recognised opera.

LIX

Not a sell inch, not a boil not a never seeking cellar.

LX

Little gem in in little gem in an. Extra.

LXI

Catch as catch as coal up.

LXII

Necklaces, neck laces, necklaces, neck laces.

LXIII

Little in in in in.

LXIV

Next or Sunday, next or sunday check.

LXV

Wide in swim, wide in swim pansy.

LXVI

Next to hear next to hear old boat seak, old boat seak
next to hear.

LXVII

Ape pail ape pail to glow.

L X V I I I

It was in on an each tuck. It was in on an each tuck.

L X I X

Wire lean string, wire lean string excellent miss on one
    pepper cute. Open so mister soil in to close not a see
    wind not seat glass.

GERTRUDE STEIN

Because words are used mainly to "make sense," it seems strange to use them in a completely different way, as Gertrude Stein did. She wrote as no one had before.

Almost always, when reading the newspaper or a novel or in everyday talking or writing, we concentrate mainly on meaning. Language has other qualities than meaning which affect us but to which we don't pay as much attention. We don't usually pay much attention, for instance, to the sound of a word, to what other words it sounds like, to whether it is a long or a short word, a solemn-sounding or crazy-sounding word. We don't think about how the sound of a word changes when it is next to other words, or about all the word's different meanings. We don't usually think much, either, about what the different sounds of talking are like—the sound of asking a question or of answering, the sound of explaining something, the sound of telling a secret, the sound of certainty or surprise or hesitation or excitement. These other qualities of language are, in general, more important in poetry than in other kinds of writing. In Gertude Stein's poetry probably more obviously than in most other poetry, she uses these other possibilities of language to make a kind of sense that seems very different from the usual kind of sense.

The "sense" of her poetry is a sense you are probably more used to in music or in abstract painting. Think, for instance, about a painting of a blue vase. You notice the vase and the blueness. But suppose a painter decides to make the blue more important. He might just paint blue and leave out the vase. In the same way that the vase might get in the way of your noticing something about blueness, meaning might get in the way of your noticing and responding to other things about language. And so a writer might leave out regular meaning as much as possible so that the words and the way they are put together can be more important parts of the sense—for the writer while he is writing the poem as well as for the reader while he is reading it. Writing in this way, it is perhaps possible to say things that couldn't be said with the usual kind of sense.

Of course, words always have meaning, no matter how you use them. If you write, "There are the saids to jelly," the words mean what they usually do. But the words used together in that way don't mean anything we already know. The sounds and meanings go together and seem to suggest something, something that doesn't become definite enough to make the regular kind of sense.

"Susie Asado" is said to be a poem about a real person, a Spanish flamenco dancer. Gertrude Stein seems to have been inspired by Susie Asado, perhaps by Susie Asado dancing. Or it could have been just the name *Susie Asado* that mainly inspired the poem. Or maybe it was something else. Anyway, this isn't a regular description of Susie Asado.

You can imagine, probably, the rather odd process of putting words together so that they sound like the way somebody or something is but so that they aren't at all descriptive; and then of finding more words, so that when you put them together, they go on sounding like the person or place or thing or, at least, they go on pleasing you and sounding somehow right. Maybe *sweet* sounds like Susie Asado. Maybe it sounds even better, or more like her, if you say it four or five times and if you follow it with *tea*: "Sweet sweet sweet sweet sweet tea." It sounds right to you. Who knows why? It sounds like the way you want to start the poem.

If the poem made more of the regular kind of sense, if it began with "How nice it is to drink a cup of tea" or

"Sweet orange pekoe tea in China cups," it would limit the poem to rather definite things. Instead, the words make a certain music, they go fast, they suddenly stop, they are emphatic, they seem to begin to suggest something, to suggest, perhaps, mysterious images or a flash of color, to suggest someone speaking softly, then that disappears and there is something else. More of the regular kind of meaning would overpower all that and make it harder to hear and see. A new way of writing means that something can be said or known that couldn't be said or known before, that there is, perhaps, some other way of thinking. Artists like to do something new. It's like being an inventor—you add something to the world that wasn't there before.

Write a poem about someone who seems to you in some sense indescribable in any regular way—a friend, someone you love, a movie star, whomever—someone with a marvelous quality you would like to put into words. Don't make sense. In a way, writing like Gertrude Stein is like making up your own language—not new words but new ways of using them and of putting them together. You might start with something that is already written— a page of a novel, for instance—and put it into lines, changing most of the words so that you can no longer tell what it's about. Think of the person while you write, but don't try to describe him at all. You might go through a dictionary and find some words that for no reason you can think of remind you of the person in some way, and then find a way to use those words in your poem. Probably the less you understand the connections, the better. Make it a rule not to use any word that actually describes the person. Remember, don't make your poem just a list of words; it should be like talking in a private language. Gertrude Stein's poems sound like someone really talking, talking in all kinds of different ways, with different attitudes, different tones of voice. Make it that way, like talking—asking questions, interrupting yourself, saying something emphatically, then maybe forgetting what you were saying, then whispering or speaking formally, as in a speech. Use lots of different kinds of words—verbs, nouns, adverbs, pronouns, and so on. Gertrude Stein uses a lot of repetition, as if she were always starting over or always coming back to some main idea. You might want to do this too. You could also try writing about a place as well as writing about a person. Keep working on the poem, changing things around, trying all kinds of things, until you've written something that you like.

Rainer Maria Rilke
(1875–1926)

Five sonnets from Sonnets to Orpheus

Mirrors, no one yet has really described
what you are in your true nature.
You, as if filled with nothing but the holes
of a sieve, the intervals of time.

You, spendthrift, still giving yourself away to the empty
    ballroom—
when the dark dawn comes, as wide as the forests,
and the chandelier goes, like a sixteen-point stag
through your impossible gateway.

Sometimes you are full of paintings.
A few seem to have entered into you—
others you sent shyly past.

But the loveliest girl will remain until,
there to her withheld cheeks,
Narcissus, clear and set free, shall force his way.

    •

Full, ripe apple, pear and banana,
gooseberry . . . all these speak

death and life in the mouth . . . I perceive . . .
Read it from a child's face

who tastes them. This comes from far away.
Is something slowly becoming nameless in your mouth?
Where once were words, discoveries flow,
startled and set free from the flesh of the fruit.

Dare to *say* what you call Apple.
This sweetness, which first condenses,
is quietly put down into the taste,

so as to become clear, thin and transparent,
ambiguous, sunny, earthy, familiar—:
oh, experience, feeling, joy—enormous!

•

Wait . . . that tastes good . . . already it is on the wing.
Just a little music, a stamping, a humming—:
girls, you warm, girls, you silent,
dance the flavor of the fruit you learned!

Dance the orange. Who can forget her,
how she, drowned in herself, still struggles
against her own sweetness. You have possessed her.
She has deliciously turned into you.

Dance the orange. The warmer landscape—
hurl it around you, so that the ripe fruit shines
in its native air. Glowing, uncover

fragrance upon fragrance! Create the relation
with the pure, resisting rind,
with the juice, with which it joyously fills!

•

Spring has come again. The earth
is like a child who has learned poems by heart,
many, oh many . . . by working long
and hard at her lessons, she has won the prize.

Her teacher was strict. We liked the white
in the beard of the old man.
Now, if we ask her to name the blues,
the greens: she can, she can!

Lucky, vacationing earth, play
now with the children. We try to catch you,
happy earth. The happiest will do it.

Oh, what her teacher has taught her—so much!
and everything that's printed in roots, and long,
difficult stems: she sings it, she sings!

•

Where, in whatever happily watered garden, on what
trees, from which tenderly stripped, leafless blossom-
    cups
ripen the strange fruits of Solace? These
exquisite fruits: perhaps you will find one in the trampled
    meadow

of your desolation. Once and then again
you marvel at the size of the fruit,
at its wholesomeness, at the softness of the skin,
and that the carelessness of the bird or the jealousy of
    the worm did not

get there first. Are there trees, then, clustered with an-
    gels

and nurtured so strangely by slow, hidden gardeners
that they bear fruit, even when we do not own them?

Have we never been able, we shadows and phantoms,
in our actions—ripe too soon and then withered again—
to disturb their impassive summer calm?

translated by Christopher Hawthorne

CHILDHOOD

The long anxiety and time of school
runs on with waiting, with nothing but dull things.
O solitude, o heavy spending of time . . .
Then out: the streets are ringing and asparkle,
and in the squares the fountains leaping,
and in the gardens the world becomes so wide.—
And to go through it all in one's small suit,
quite differently than others go and used to go—:
O wonderful strange time, o spending of time,
o solitude.

And to look out far away into it all:
men and women; men, men, women
and children who are different and gay-colored;
and there a house and now and then a dog
and terror changing soundlessly to trust—:
O sorrow without meaning, o dream, o dread,
o groundless deep.

And so to play: ball and ring and hoop
in a garden that is gently paling,

and sometimes to brush against the grownups,
blind and disheveled in the haste of tag,
but in the evening quietly, with small stiff
steps to go walking home, firmly held on to—:
O ever more elusive understanding,
o fear, o burden.

And for hours on end beside the big gray pond
to kneel with a little sailing boat;
to forget it because still other sails
like it and finer are drawing through the circles,
and to have to think of that small pale
face that sinking shone out of the pond—:
O childhood, o images slipping from us.
Whither? Whither?

translated by M. D. Herter Norton

RAINER MARIA RILKE

For the most part, people get used to the way things are and to the explanations for the way things are. There are, in fact, many different kinds of explanations: scientific, philosophical, historical, psychological, theological, and so on. Poetry is often concerned with another kind of understanding. It has less to do with getting to the absolute truth with facts or logic or faith or proof. It has more to do with what things seem to be, with what they mean to you, with what they are in your thoughts and feelings and imagination, where things remain a little mysterious. In your imagination, a tree isn't just any tree in nature —it's also affected by your own life, your feelings, your associations, your memories; maybe, for instance, you can identify with it in one way or another, imagining that it is something like you. Rilke writes about this other life that things have in our thoughts.

Rainer Maria Rilke was a German poet who lived from 1875 to 1926. The five sonnets here are from a series of fifty-five sonnets that he wrote within a few weeks when he was very inspired. He called the series *Sonnets to Orpheus.* Orpheus was a mythical poet who had a magical relationship with things: his songs caused objects to begin to listen and to speak. Rilke must have felt a little like Orpheus when he wrote these poems. Feeling mysteriously inspired, he, like Orpheus, has a special relationship with things. They seem to reveal to him their hidden natures. Rilke perceives, for instance, the "true being" of mirrors. The mirror helplessly devotes itself to whatever is in front of it, even empty ballrooms. Some things disappear into the gigantic emptiness of the mirror; other things the mirror sends away. Narcissus is caught there, but perhaps someday will go out of it to the beautiful girl who stays looking in the mirror, neither disappearing into it nor going away.

When Rilke writes about a subject, it is as if nothing were known about it, as if he started from the very beginning in order to understand deeply, for himself, the power or purpose or beauty of it. Mirrors, the taste of fruit, the sound of an instrument or of a bird's cry, the feeling of grief or of solace—they are all new and startling. The true being of the thing he is writing about has been kept silently within it, as in a secret memory, which he somehow guesses: spring is the beautiful and difficult lesson that the earth has been memorizing all winter; the tastes of different fruits are really amazing stories that these fruits are telling us about faraway places; the secret origin of solace is in trees in faraway orchards that are tended by angels.

Rilke seems, by identifying with these things, to come to a strange kind of understanding of them. Think of how it is possible to identify with and understand a person you don't know very well, imagining his life, imagining what it is that he feels and thinks and wants. What you imagined would not be literally true and you wouldn't expect it to be. It would come from what you knew about the person, and from your knowledge of and ideas about other people in general, and from your knowledge of yourself. It would have something to do with you and something to do with the person you were thinking about. It would perhaps be something like what you would be like if you were that person.

It is possible to identify with and "understand" a mirror in almost that same way. The true being of the mirror that Rilke writes about is probably connected to his own experience of mirrors. His poem connects mirrors with his own ideas about them—with ballrooms, paintings, and beautiful girls, and also with water and the Greek story of Narcissus, a beautiful boy who fell in love with his reflection in a pool and drowned trying to get close to it. His conception of a mirror also probably has something to do with what he imagines he would be like if he himself were a mirror—reflecting whatever is in front of him, absorbing some things, rejecting others and identifying himself with the image (reflection) of Narcissus trapped in the pool and wanting to be free of himself and with a beautiful girl. We don't know all the connections, nor perhaps did Rilke when he wrote the poem. But of course one doesn't need to understand them in order to like the poem.

It may seem strange to write with this kind of intense concern about the lives of things that don't really have lives. But if you forget your knowledge of what is possible, it isn't hard to imagine what it would be like to be a screen door, with that construction, that density, that way of moving, of being still, to imagine its secret life— its habits, intentions, dreams, wishes, memories. You can imagine, in the same way, the creation and purpose of a dog's bark, the history of gravity, the country in which Indifference was born and brought up. You might want to choose as your subject something with which you secretly sympathize or identify. Don't let there be logical connections between the subject and what you write about it. If you write about a screen door or the force of gravity, you might try thinking of it as having a secret mission in the world—and a secret sorrow and pain. No matter how strange they seem, act as if the facts you are inventing are really facts. Be simple, particular, and sure of what you say, the way you would be if you were explaining the personality of a peculiar or astonishing friend. It is fine if the subject, after the poem is finished, is still mysterious.

Wallace Stevens
(1879–1955)

DISILLUSIONMENT OF TEN O'CLOCK

The houses are haunted
By white night-gowns.
None are green,
Or purple with green rings,
Or green with yellow rings,
Or yellow with blue rings.
None of them are strange,
With socks of lace
And beaded ceintures.
People are not going
To dream of baboons and periwinkles.
Only, here and there, an old sailor,
Drunk and asleep in his boots,
Catches tigers
In red weather.

THIRTEEN WAYS OF LOOKING
AT A BLACKBIRD

I

Among twenty snowy mountains,
The only moving thing
Was the eye of the blackbird.

II

I was of three minds,
Like a tree
In which there are three blackbirds.

III

The blackbird whirled in the autumn winds.
It was a small part of the pantomime.

IV

A man and a woman
Are one.
A man and a woman and a blackbird
Are one.

V

I do not know which to prefer,
The beauty of inflections
Or the beauty of innuendoes,
The blackbird whistling
Or just after.

VI

Icicles filled the long window
With barbaric glass.
The shadow of the blackbird

Crossed it, to and fro.
The mood
Traced in the shadow
An indecipherable cause.

VII

O thin men of Haddam,
Why do you imagine golden birds?
Do you not see how the blackbird
Walks around the feet
Of the women about you?

VIII

I know noble accents
And lucid, inescapable rhythms;
But I know, too,
That the blackbird is involved
In what I know.

IX

When the blackbird flew out of sight,
It marked the edge
Of one of many circles.

X

At the sight of blackbirds
Flying in a green light,
Even the bawds of euphony
Would cry out sharply.

XI

He rode over Connecticut
In a glass coach.
Once, a fear pierced him,

In that he mistook
The shadow of his equipage
For blackbirds.

XII
The river is moving.
The blackbird must be flying.

XIII
It was evening all afternoon.
It was snowing
And it was going to snow.
The blackbird sat
In the cedar-limbs.

METAPHORS OF A MAGNIFICO

Twenty men crossing a bridge,
Into a village,
Are twenty men crossing twenty bridges,
Into twenty villages.

Or one man
Crossing a single bridge into a village.

This is old song
That will not declare itself . . .

Twenty men crossing a bridge,
Into a village,
Are

Twenty men crossing a bridge
Into a village.

That will not declare itself
Yet is certain as meaning . . .

The boots of the men clump
On the boards of the bridge.
The first white wall of the village
Rises through fruit-trees.
Of what was it I was thinking?
So the meaning escapes.

The first white wall of the village . .
The fruit-trees . . .

DEPRESSION BEFORE SPRING

The cock crows
But no queen rises.

The hair of my blonde
Is dazzling,
As the spittle of cows
Threading the wind.

Ho! Ho!

But ki-ki-ri-ki
Brings no rou-cou,

No rou-cou-cou.
But no queen comes
In slipper green.

PLOUGHING
ON SUNDAY

The white cock's tail
Tosses in the wind.
The turkey-cock's tail
Glitters in the sun.

Water in the fields.
The wind pours down.
The feathers flare
And bluster in the wind.

Remus, blow your horn!
I'm ploughing on Sunday,
Ploughing North America.
Blow your horn!

Tum-ti-tum,
Ti-tum-tum-tum!
The turkey-cock's tail
Spreads to the sun.

The white cock's tail
Streams to the moon.
Water in the fields.
The wind pours down.

ANECDOTE OF THE JAR

I placed a jar in Tennessee,
And round it was, upon a hill.
It made the slovenly wilderness
Surround that hill.

The wilderness rose up to it,
And sprawled around, no longer wild.
The jar was round upon the ground
And tall and of a port in air.

It took dominion everywhere.
The jar was gray and bare.
It did not give of bird or bush,
Like nothing else in Tennessee.

GUBBINAL

That strange flower, the sun,
Is just what you say.
Have it your way.

The world is ugly,
And the people are sad.

That tuft of jungle feathers,
That animal eye,
Is just what you say.

That savage of fire,
That seed,
Have it your way.

The world is ugly,
And the people are sad.

ANECDOTE
OF THE PRINCE
OF PEACOCKS

In the moonlight
I met Berserk,
In the moonlight
On the bushy plain.
Oh, sharp he was
As the sleepless!

And, "Why are you red
In this milky blue?"
I said.
"Why sun-colored,
As if awake
In the midst of sleep?"

"You that wander,"
So he said,
"On the bushy plain,
Forget so soon.
But I set my traps
In the midst of dreams."

I knew from this
That the blue ground
Was full of blocks
And blocking steel.
I knew the dread
Of the bushy plain,
And the beauty
Of the moonlight
Falling there,
Falling
As sleep falls
In the innocent air.

THE BRAVE MAN

The sun, that brave man,
Comes through boughs that lie in wait,
That brave man.

Green and gloomy eyes
In dark forms of the grass
Run away.

The good stars,
Pale helms and spiky spurs,
Run away.

Fears of my bed,
Fears of life and fears of death,
Run away.

That brave man comes up
From below and walks without meditation,
That brave man.

A RABBIT AS KING
OF THE GHOSTS

The difficulty to think at the end of day,
When the shapeless shadow covers the sun
And nothing is left except light on your fur—

There was the cat slopping its milk all day,
Fat cat, red tongue, green mind, white milk
And August the most peaceful month.

To be, in the grass, in the peacefullest time,
Without that monument of cat,
The cat forgotten in the moon;

And to feel that the light is a rabbit-light,
In which everything is meant for you
And nothing need be explained;

Then there is nothing to think of. It comes of itself;
And east rushes west and west rushes down,
No matter. The grass is full

And full of yourself. The trees around are for you,
The whole of the wideness of night is for you,
A self that touches all edges,

You become a self that fills the four corners of night.
The red cat hides away in the fur-light
And there you are humped high, humped up,

You are humped higher and higher, black as stone—
You sit with your head like a carving in space
And the little green cat is a bug in the grass.

WALLACE STEVENS

One of the first things you notice in Wallace Stevens's poetry is how full of bright, gorgeous things it is—fruit trees, feathers, red weather, elegant gestures, beautiful clothes, delightful-sounding words. This has something to do with Wallace Stevens's ideas. He had, in fact, very strong ideas about what things were like, how people should look at them, think of them, and write poems about them. In his later poems, he often wrote about these ideas. He thought the world, if you saw it as it really was, was beautiful and dazzling, that you could be constantly discovering its amazing beauty if you gave what you were looking at all your attention, using your imagination, seeing it as if for the first time, seeing everything always in a new way. He thought this was the most exhilarating, most joyful, best, and truest way to see anything, to think of it, to write of it. It's more comfortable to see and think of everything in the same old way. People are very drawn to what is familiar. It seems easiest if it is all known in advance, if everything always makes the same kind of sense and nothing is unusual or unexpected. But that keeps you from discovering the beauty all around you. It keeps you from the new things that you could see and think and say.

Stevens's idea was that even simple, plain things, like a blackbird or a plowed field, are exotic and amazing. Think, for example, of the rain. You look out the window and it is raining. You think, "I need my umbrella today." You're used to the rain. You look at it; but in a way you don't really see it. But what if it were the first rain you ever saw? If you didn't know what it was? If you could forget, for a minute, everything except the rain? How would it look and smell and feel and sound? What would you think or write about it? Wallace Stevens thought that it was possible to look at things that way, that we have a choice about the way things are, and that what they are depends on our own imaginations. He thought that poetry wasn't a way to figure out and give order to the past, but a way to start again, to begin something new. You start with nothing except what is there; with no idea except what you are just beginning to think. The poems are not about eternal truth but about the truth of the surface of things, the truth of the way things have just begun to be.

"The poem," he said in one of his poems, "refreshes the world." He thought words were a way of expanding the senses—that is, words were a way of discovering things, and of making them new. To describe the sun as a "savage of fire" is to see it as if for the first time; to describe it as an "animal eye" is to see it for the first time again.

Stevens's poems, in their exuberance about refreshing the world, are full of colors and full of all kinds of details of shape and hardness and softness and fragrance and smoothness and shine and coolness and elegance and warmth and sound. They are full, too, of all kinds of strange-sounding, unfamiliar words (*ceintures, periwinkles*) and phrases (*slipper green, bawds of euphony, barbaric glass*) and, sometimes, sound imitations (*rou-cou-cou* and *tum-ti-tum*). There is a richness in the way the poems sound. There is a lot of alliteration ("The houses are haunted," "But no queen comes"), and rhyming sounds are scattered throughout ("In red weather," "By white nightgowns").

In "Disillusionment of Ten O'Clock," Stevens is writing about people who don't use their imaginations. He makes the poem funny and sensuous by talking mostly about what they are *not* wearing to bed, and what they are *not* going to dream. In Stevens's view, they're missing a lot, in contrast to the sailor who, although he may be drunk, is better off because he at least is having exciting dreams—his imagination isn't dead.

Write a poem like "Disillusionment of Ten O'Clock." Try starting with the ordinary way things actually are— say what things people are wearing, for instance, or doing or building or carrying or saying. But make most of the poem about the way things are not. You can make the poem about the world in general or about a particular place or group of people—your school, your house, your block, your city, your state; teachers, parents, bus drivers, doctors, politicians. Write what people are not going to wear, what they're not going to think of or talk about or dream of, what the buildings do not look like, what colors or shapes things do not have. Make this "not" part of the poem very sensuous and particular and extravagant: balloons and banners, for example, are not in the windows, policemen are not dressed in golden armor and directing traffic with bugles and gongs, classrooms are not in the shapes of stars or of hearts, houses are not being built in the clouds. Try using very beautiful or very strange-sounding words, words you've never used before. You might go through a dictionary and find some. Or make up some sounds like *rou-cou-cou.* You can use alliteration, too, and internal rhyme—whatever makes the sound of the poem rich and interesting.

Another kind of poem to write is one like "Thirteen Ways of Looking at a Blackbird." In each stanza of this poem, the blackbird is different because of a different way of seeing it—it has a different place in the world, a different place in Stevens's imagination. In the first stanza Stevens sees the blackbird as if in a black-and-white movie, with everything around it white and still—only its eye is moving. In the second stanza he sees the blackbird as part of a comparison: his three contrasting opinions are like three blackbirds. The third stanza has the blackbird whirling in the wind as if it were part of a theatrical performance, a pantomime show. In the fourth stanza it is part of a philosophical proposition; in the fifth, the subject of a speculation about music; in the sixth, part of a frightening story; in the seventh, like something in the Prophets part of the Bible; in the eighth, part of a statement about psychology; in the ninth, like something in mathematics. The tenth stanza talks about the kind of music the sight of blackbirds would inspire. The eleventh stanza sounds like something from an old novel—here blackbirds are only inside someone's feelings as part of a fear. The twelfth stanza is like nature lore, something a farmer would know. The last stanza is, again, like a black-and-white movie, but different from the first time: here the blackbird is completely still and it is the white snow that moves.

Write this poem about something rather ordinary—an orange, a window, clouds, fir trees, a cat, a lake, whatever. Your poem can be in three parts or five or six or ten or thirteen or fifty. Begin again with each new part, thinking about the subject in a new way—the way it is in summer, in winter, in your thoughts, in your dreams, up close, far away, in the rain, in the dark, in your memories, in China, in the desert, in outer space, moving or very still. Think of it too, perhaps, as part of some other subject you know about—maybe music or chemistry or physics. Or think of it as it would appear in a newspaper article, a story, an autobiography, a history book, an essay. Each time, imagine everything very clearly and particularly. Some parts can be shorter, some parts longer. Don't try to make the parts go together in some way or another or try to come to some conclusion at the end. Thirteen ways of imagining a subject should be a little like having thirteen different subjects.

Guillaume Apollinaire
(1880–1918)

ZONE

You're tired of this old world at last

The flock of bridges is bleating this morning O shep-
herdess Eiffel Tower

You've had enough of living in the Greek and Roman
past

Even the cars look ancient here
Only religion has stayed new religion
Has stayed simple like the hangars at Port-Aviation

O Christianity you alone in Europe are not ancient
The most modern European is you Pope Pius X
And you whom the windows observe shame forbids this
morning
Your going into a church and confessing
You read the handbills the catalogs the posters that
really sing
That's poetry and there are newspapers if you want
prose this morning

There are dime serials filled with detective stories
Portraits of great men and a thousand other categories

This morning I saw a pretty street whose name I have
    forgotten
Clean and new it was the bugle of the sun
The managers the workers and the beautiful secretaries
From Monday morning to Saturday afternoon go by four
    times a day
Each morning the whistle wails three times
About noon a clock barks out twelve angry chimes
The words written on signs and walls
Like squawking parrots the plaques and Post No Bills
I love the charm of this industrial street
Located in Paris between the rue Aumont-Thiéville and
    the avenue des Ternes

That's the young street and you are still just a boy
Your mother dresses you in blue and white only
You are highly devout and with your oldest friend René
    Dalize
You love nothing so much as the church ceremonies
It's nine o'clock the gas is down all blue you tiptoe out
    of the dormitory
You pray all night in the school oratory
While the eternal and adorable deep amethyst
Turns forever the flaming glory of Christ
It's the beautiful lily we all grow
It's the red-haired torch the wind does not blow out
It's the pale and bright red son of the sorrowful mother
It's the tree with all prayers evergreen in all weather
It's the double beam of honor and eternity
It's the six-sided star
It's God who dies on Friday and is resurrected on Sunday
It's Christ who goes up in the sky better than any pilot
    could

He holds the world's record for altitude
Pupil Christ of the eye
Twentieth pupil of the centuries he knows how to do it
    there
And changed into a bird this century like Jesus rises in
    the air
The devils in the depths look up to see a
Thing they say imitates Simon Magus in Judea
"If he can fly he surely flies by night!"
The angels flip and fly around the handsome acrobat
Icarus Enoch Elie Apollonius of Tyana
Glide around the first airplane
Sometimes they part for the carriers of the Holy Eucha-
    rist
Those priests who rise eternally in elevating the host
At last the plane alights but doesn't fold its wings
The sky is then filled with a million flying things
The crows the owls the falcons swirl and dive
The ibises the flamingos the marabous from Africa arrive
The roc which poets and storytellers have celebrated
Glides clutching Adam's skull the first head
Over the horizon the eagle's swooping cry is heard
And from America comes the little hummingbird
From China come the pihis long and supple
Which have only one wing and fly in couples
Then the dove spirit immaculate
With an oscillated peacock and lyrebird escort
The pyre that begets its own self the phoenix
Like glowing coals which turn back into sticks
Leaving behind the perilous straits all three
Sirens arrive singing beautifully
And all eagle phoenix and pihis from China fraternize
With the machine moving across the skies

Now you walk in Paris alone in the crowd
Herds of buses drive past mooing loud

Your throat is gripped with love's pain
As if you should never be loved again
If you lived in the past you'd enter a monastery
You're ashamed to catch yourself saying a prayer
You jeer at yourself and your laughter crackles like
    hellfire
The background of your life is gilded by the sparks from
    your laughter
It's like paintings hung in a somber museum
Sometimes you step up close to see them

Today you walk in Paris the women are all bloodstained
It was and I'd rather not remember it was beauty on the
    wane

Surrounded with fervent flames Notre-Dame looked
    down at me in Chartres
The blood of your Sacré-Coeur flooded me in Mont-
    martre
I'm sick of hearing blessed speeches
The love I suffer from is a shameful sickness
And all night the agonizing image whispers in your ear
That passing image is always near

Now you hear the Mediterranean's sound
Beneath the lemon trees blooming all year round
With your friends you go out on the sea
One from Nice one Mentonasque and two from La Tur-
    bie
The octopi from the depths fill our hearts with fear
And among the algae the fish swim symbols of the Savior

You're in the garden of an inn outside of Prague
You feel so happy a rose is on the table
And instead of writing your story in prose
You watch the beetle sleeping in the heart of the rose

In the agates of St. Vitus you see a drawing of your face
It was a horribly depressing and frightening place
You're like Lazarus utterly terrified by the light of day
The hands of the clock in the Jewish quarter turn the
    wrong way
And you too move back slowly through your life going
Up to Hradcany and through the evening listening
To them singing Czech songs in the taverns

Here you are in Marseilles among the watermelons

Here you are in Coblenz at the Hotel Gnome

Here you are sitting under a Japanese loquat tree in
    Rome

Here you are in Amsterdam with a girl that you find
    beautiful and who is a hag
She's supposed to marry a student at Den Haag
Where they rent students rooms in Latin Cubicula
    Locanda
I remember it I spent three days there and three more
    in Gouda

You go before the examining magistrate in Paris
Like a criminal you are placed under arrest
Your travels were both sad and spectacular
Before you realized what deceit and aging are
At twenty and thirty your love affairs were cruel
I've wasted my time and I've lived like a fool
You don't dare look at your hands anymore and you
    constantly feel like crying
Over yourself over her whom I love over everything ter-
    rifying

These poor immigrants fill your eyes with tears
They nurse their young they believe in God and prayers
Their smell fills the hall of the Gare Saint-Lazare
Like the Three Kings they have faith in their star
They hope to take on finer airs in Buenos Aires
And return successful in business affairs
One family carries a red comforter the way you carry
    your heart
That comforter and our dreams are equally unreal
Some of the immigrants move in here and stay
In hovels on the rue des Ecouffes or rue des Rosiers
I've often seen them taking the evening air
Like chess pieces they generally just sit there
Mostly Jews their women sit ghost white
Deep in their shops in wigs all day and night

You stand at the counter in some low-down café
With wretches you have a cheap cup of coffee

You're in a big restaurant at night

These women are all right they have their plight
Still all even her have hurt their lovers and she's a fright

She's the daughter of a policeman on the Isle of Jersey

I hadn't seen her hard chapped hands sticking out of her
    jersey

I feel horribly sorry for the scars on her belly

Now I humiliate to a poor girl with a horrible laugh my
    mouth

You're alone morning's on its way
The milkmen bang their cans in the street

Night slips away like a lovely half-breed
It's false Ferdine or attentive Lea

And you drink this alcohol that burns like your spirit
Your spirit you drink down like spirits

You walk toward Auteuil you want to go home on foot
To sleep among fetishes from Oceania and Guinea which
    put
Christ in another form with other inspirations
They are inferior Christs of dark aspirations

Goodbye and God keep you

Sun throat cut

translated by Ron Padgett

THE LITTLE CAR

The 31st day of August 1914
I left Deauville a little before midnight
In Rouveyre's little car

With his driver there were three of us

We said goodbye to an entire epoch
Furious giants were rising over Europe

The eagles were leaving their aeries expecting the sun
The voracious fish were rising from the depths
The masses were rushing toward some deeper under-
standing
The dead were trembling with fear in their dark dwell-
ings

The dogs were barking toward over there where the
frontiers are
I went bearing within me all those armies fighting
I felt them rise up in me and spread out over the coun-
tries they wound through
With the forests the happy villages of Belgium
Francorchamps with l'Eau Rouge and the mineral
springs
Region where the invasions always take place
Railway arteries where those who were going to die
Saluted one last time this colorful life
Deep oceans where monsters were moving
In old shipwrecked hulks
Unimaginable heights where man fights
Higher than the eagle soars
There man fights man
And falls like a shooting star
I felt in myself new and totally capable beings
Build and organize a new universe
A merchant of amazing opulence and astounding size
Was laying out an extraordinary display
And gigantic shepherds were leading
Great silent flocks that were browsing on words
With every dog along the road barking at them

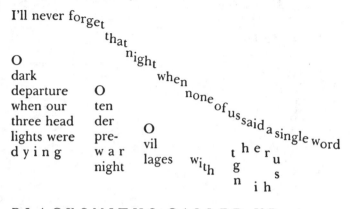

I'll never forget
that
night
O
dark   when
departure   O   none of us said a single word
when our   ten
three head   der   O   the
lights were pre-   vil   r u
d y i n g   w a r   lages   with   t g   s
             night   n   i h

BLACKSMITHS CALLED UP
between midnight and one o'clock in the morning

        to   sil
     v e r   V e r
   y b l u e   or else   V e r
     L i s i   s a i l
     eux   les
and 3 times we stopped to change a tire that had blown out

And when having passed that afternoon
Through Fontainebleau
We arrived in Paris
Just as the mobilization posters were going up
We understood my buddy and I
That the little car had taken us into a new epoch
And although we were both grown men
We had just been born

translated by Ron Padgett, with help from Keith Cohen, LeRoy C.
Breunig, Michel Décaudin, and Patricia Padgett

IT'S RAINING

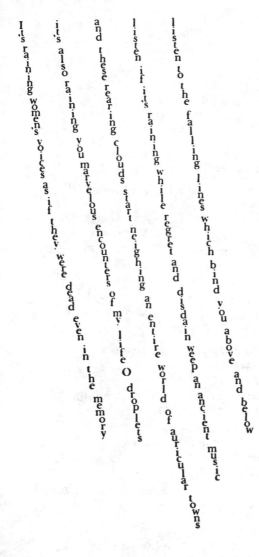

It's raining women's voices as if they were dead even in the memory

it's also raining you marvelous encounters of my life O droplets

and these rearing clouds start neighing an entire world of auricular towns

listen if it's raining while regret and disdain weep an ancient music

listen to the falling lines which bind you above and below

GUILLAUME APOLLINAIRE

The French poet Guillaume Apollinaire lived and wrote at the end of the nineteenth and the beginning of the twentieth century. He was killed in World War I. His lifetime corresponded with the beginning of modern times, of the modern world, the world of automobiles, airplanes, electricity, and modern cities. He was twenty years old when the twentieth century started. It was a time of general excitement, with the beginning of the new century making people think of and be excited about all kinds of newness and change. And Apollinaire lived in Paris, the most beautiful city of the world, the city that was the center of art and science and thought, where it seemed that everything that mattered was going on. More than other poets, Apollinaire seemed to feel, and was able to express in his poems, the spirit and the excitement of the new time. His poems are full of praise for the beauty of modern things—airport hangars, newspapers, billboards, new industrial streets—and, like life in a modern city, the poems are often fragmented and rapidly changing. He was moved by the beauty of airplanes as other poets were moved by the beauty of roses. He was also moved by roses. What he found in the new century, and in modern Paris, was not something harsh and mechanical and unpoetic but a new simplicity, variety, and beauty, like that of the "pretty industrial street." Walking around Paris, as he does in his poem "Zone," inspired him in the way poets have usually been inspired by walking around in nature.

New kinds of experiences not only give poets and other artists new subjects for their work but also often inspire them to find new forms for it, new ways of writing, different ways of painting. The excitement about the modern did this in all the arts. The Cubist painters, for example, whom Apollinaire was friends with and whose work he very much admired, painted pictures like none that had been seen before—showing things from different viewpoints at once, and full of angles and flatness, more like a modern street than, say, a meadow. Like Cubist paintings, Apollinaire's work was new and unconventional. There's no punctuation; when there is rhyme, it is so light and flat it is hardly noticeable, although sometimes it seems that the rhyme has, in fact, inspired the line; the style is often very conversational and plain; the poem often shifts from one place and time and subject to another. Apollinaire's most obviously radical modern invention in poetry is the form he calls *calligramme* (the word seems related to Oriental picture-writing, *calligraphy*, and also to *telegram*). Instead of the usual shape of poetry, the poem has a shape determined by its subject. The letters of a love poem form the outline of a heart; the letters of a poem about rain fall like raindrops from the top to the bottom of the page. Such poems not only don't read like other poems, they don't even look like them.

"It's Raining" is a rain of words, a rain of letters of words, and also a rain of memories and feelings. These lines of falling rain are curved a little bit to the right, as if blown by a gentle spring breeze. The rain makes Apollinaire think of the past, of the women he has known. It may be the soft sound of the rain that makes him think of their voices. Then he thinks of "marvelous meetings," probably meetings with the women he has loved. Then, probably looking at the sky, he sees the "crooked clouds" and hears thunder, and its roar reminds him of the roar of cities he has been in, with their noises of traffic, of people, of machines. All these things are gone now, only memories brought back by the rain. The rain binds him to the sky, where the rain begins; and to the past, where his memories begin. It binds him also to the present and to the earth, where he really is now, alone and in the rain. And the falling letters of the poem (and the raindrops too) look like a rope or a chain.

A sudden change in the weather often brings back memories. The first snow, the first warm day, can seem to bring back other snows and other warm days when you were younger and things were different. It can seem, as in Apollinaire's *calligramme,* that the memories and the weather are all part of the same thing.

To write a *calligramme,* begin with the shape of something and let that shape suggest to you what to write. In Apollinaire's *calligramme,* he doesn't write about rain in general; he writes about a particular rainy day, when he has certain feelings and certain memories. Try making your poem particular in that way. For instance, if your poem is in the shape of clouds, let the clouds be the clouds of a certain day when you looked at them and thought and said and did certain things, and let your poem be about those clouds and that day. If the poem is in the shape of a telephone, maybe you could write it about a certain conversation. If it's in the shape of a window, it might be a particular window in your house that you always look out of, waiting or thinking. A nice thing that happens in writing *calligrammes* is that the shape of the poem and the subject of the poem become mixed up and seem the same. You may want to write several.

You could also write a poem like "Zone," about walking around in a city, bringing in all kinds of things you see and the thoughts, impressions, and feelings they suggest. When you take a walk, what you feel and think is usually partly inspired by where you happen to be and what you see—a church may make you think of Sundays when you were a child; someone carrying a red comforter may make you think of yourself carrying around your sad heart. Talk to yourself in the poem, as Apollinaire does in "Zone," and let yourself be reminded of different experiences, different places, different times. Let the different parts of the city get into your poem as you come to them in your walk.

William Carlos Williams
(1883–1963)

NANTUCKET

Flowers through the window
lavender and yellow

changed by white curtains—
Smell of cleanliness—

Sunshine of late afternoon—
On the glass tray

a glass pitcher, the tumbler
turned down, by which

a key is lying—And the
immaculate white bed

THE RED WHEELBARROW

so much depends
upon

a red wheel
barrow

glazed with rain
water

beside the white
chickens.

TO A POOR OLD WOMAN

munching a plum on
the street a paper bag
of them in her hand

They taste good to her
They taste good
to her. They taste
good to her

You can see it by
the way she gives herself
to the one half
sucked out in her hand

Comforted
a solace of ripe plums
seeming to fill the air
They taste good to her

THE
LOCUST TREE
IN FLOWER

Among
of
green

stiff
old
bright

broken
branch
come

white
sweet
May

again

BETWEEN WALLS

the back wings
of the

hospital where
nothing

will grow lie
cinders

in which shine
the broken

pieces of a green
bottle

THIS IS
JUST TO SAY

I have eaten
the plums
that were in
the icebox

and which
you were probably
saving
for breakfast

Forgive me
they were delicious
so sweet
and so cold

JANUARY MORNING

SUITE:

I

I have discovered that most of
the beauties of travel are due to
the strange hours we keep to see them:

the domes of the Church of
the Paulist Fathers in Weehawken
against a smoky dawn—the heart stirred—
are beautiful as Saint Peters
approached after years of anticipation.

II

Though the operation was postponed
I saw the tall probationers
in their tan uniforms
                    hurrying to breakfast!

III

—and from basement entries
neatly coiffed, middle aged gentlemen
with orderly moustaches and
well-brushed coats

IV

—and the sun, dipping into the avenues
streaking the tops of
the irregular red houselets,
                              and
the gay shadows dropping and dropping.

V

—and a young horse with a green bed-quilt
on his withers shaking his head:
bared teeth and nozzle high in the air!

VI

—and a semicircle of dirt-colored men
about a fire bursting from an old
ash can,

VII

              —and the worn,
blue car rails (like the sky!)
gleaming among the cobbles!

VIII

—and the rickety ferry-boat "Arden"!
What an object to be called "Arden"
among the great piers,—on the
ever new river!
              "Put me a Touchstone
at the wheel, white gulls, and we'll
follow the ghost of the *Half Moon*
to the North West Passage—and through!
(at Albany!) for all that!"

XII

Long yellow rushes bending
above the white snow patches;
purple and gold ribbon
of the distant wood:
　　　　　what an angle
you make with each other as
you lie there in contemplation.

XIII

Work hard all your young days
and they'll find you too, some morning
staring up under
your chiffonier at its warped
bass-wood bottom and your soul—
out!
—among the little sparrows
behind the shutter.

XIV

—and the flapping flags are at
half mast for the dead admiral.

XV

All this—
　　　　　was for you, old woman.
I wanted to write a poem
that you would understand.
For what good is it to me
if you can't understand it?
　　　　　But you got to try hard—
But—
　　Well, you know how
the young girls run giggling

on Park Avenue after dark
when they ought to be home in bed?
Well,
that's the way it is with me somehow.

THE ACT

There were the roses, in the rain.
Don't cut them, I pleaded.
    They won't last, she said
But they're so beautiful
    where they are.
Agh, we were all beautiful once, she
    said,
and cut them and gave them to me
    in my hand.

THE LAST WORDS
OF MY ENGLISH
GRANDMOTHER

There were some dirty plates
and a glass of milk
beside her on a small table
near the rank, disheveled bed—

Wrinkled and nearly blind
she lay and snored
rousing with anger in her tones
to cry for food,

Gimme something to eat—
They're starving me—
I'm all right I won't go
to the hospital. No, no, no

Give me something to eat
Let me take you
to the hospital, I said
and after you are well

you can do as you please.
She smiled, Yes
you do what you please first
then I can do what I please—

Oh, oh, oh! she cried
as the ambulance men lifted
her to the stretcher—
Is this what you call

making me comfortable?
By now her mind was clear—
Oh you think you're smart
you young people,

she said, but I'll tell you
you don't know anything.
Then we started.
On the way

we passed a long row
of elms. She looked at them
awhile out of
the ambulance window and said,

What are all those
fuzzy-looking things out there?
Trees? Well, I'm tired
of them and rolled her head away.

WILLIAM CARLOS WILLIAMS

William Carlos Williams, more than any other poet, brought the plain, ordinary things of twentieth-century America and also its plain, everyday talk into poetry. Sometimes people have the idea that the subjects of poems have to be worthy of poetry—by being special enough, beautiful enough, profound enough, emotional enough. Or they have the idea that a simple subject has to be elevated and transformed by ideas, by secret significance, and so on, before it is really a poem.

Such ideas about poetry make the poems of Williams Carlos Williams a surprise. Williams's poetry is, for the most part, written in plain language about ordinary things—ordinary places, ordinary people, ordinary conversations, ordinary days. He writes about broken glass in an alley, a woman eating plums from a paper bag, a wheelbarrow, a room in an inn. All these are things that he likes. People are moved by things that are officially beautiful, like roses and the moon; they are also moved by things that aren't usually considered beautiful—neon signs, old stairways, yards, rusty bicycles.

Williams writes about ordinary things with excitement and attention. He looks at what happens to be around him the way a scholar might look at a great work of art. It is as if every detail were a genius stroke. And so it is important to describe everything with perfect exactitude, to get it all just right—the shine of the glass, the white curtains, the half-sucked-out plum in the old woman's hand. To get everything right means, for one thing, getting just the right words. For Williams the best words seem to be the plain, common, particular ones. And these work best when they have the sound of the way people usually say them, the music of ordinary talk:

"They taste/good to her." "Forgive me/they were delicious." "They won't last, she said."

Williams usually writes about things just as they are, without added philosophy or scenery or feelings. His poems are most often divided into very short lines, as if he wanted to separate the details, to put enough space between them so that nothing, however simple and unimportant-seeming, would be lost.

There are probably many things which you like but which you don't think are important enough to write poems about, or maybe even to talk about—things you like to wear or think of or look at which are generally not considered at all beautiful or inspiring. Almost always, people can think of a place, for instance, where they like very much to be, although they may not be able to say exactly why—perhaps a place where they can be alone just to think or to daydream, a certain part of a yard or a park, a room, a particular beach. Maybe it's a place you have been to only once—someone's garden, or a hotel room, as in Williams's poem "Nantucket," where you stayed during a vacation. Write a poem about such a place. Be very simple and particular. Make it all just the place, nothing extra—no memories, feelings, ideas. Close your eyes and imagine you're there. What do you see first? What afterward? You might put down different details of the place just in the order you remember them, one in each line. Describe them in the plainest way. Use short lines and leave spaces. It will probably be a better poem if you don't try to make a point and if you don't try to make it "poetic." A good title might be the name of the town or the road where the place is.

Another kind of poem to write is a poem with only one word in each line, like Williams's "The Locust Tree in Flower." Williams's poem doesn't make sense as a regular sentence ("Among of green stiff old . . .") nor is it a list of purely descriptive words. Still, there isn't anything mysterious about it; the title makes it perfectly clear what it's about.

Write a poem like this in which you look at or think about something, and keep registering your impression of it in one one-word line after another. One way to do this that will help you get away from having only a regular sentence is to make it a rule that you can't think of any word in advance; make each one a new and separate statement. Don't let it be just a list of descriptive adjectives and nouns. Include some adverbs, verbs, and prepositions. Some, or perhaps many, of the words that occur to you may not seem to you connected to the subject in any obvious way. That's fine. When all the words are read together, they will probably have a different effect. Try using a title long enough to show what your poem is about.

D. H. Lawrence
(1885–1930)

BUTTERFLY

Butterfly, the wind blows sea-ward, strong beyond the
    garden wall!
Butterfly, why do you settle on my shoe, and sip the dirt
    on my shoe,
Lifting your veined wings, lifting them? big white but-
    terfly!

Already it is October, and the wind blows strong to the
    sea
from the hills where snow must have fallen, the wind is
    polished with snow.
Here in the garden, with red geraniums, it is warm, it is
    warm
but the wind blows strong to sea-ward, white butterfly,
    content on my shoe!

Will you go, will you go from my warm house?
Will you climb on your big soft wings, black-dotted,
as up an invisible rainbow, an arch
till the wind slides you sheer from the arch-crest
and in a strange level fluttering you go out to sea-ward,
    white speck!

Farewell, farewell, lost soul!
you have melted in the crystalline distance,
it is enough! I saw you vanish into air.

BAVARIAN GENTIANS

Not every man has gentians in his house
in soft September, at slow, sad Michaelmas.

Bavarian gentians, big and dark, only dark
darkening the day-time, torch-like with the smoking
    blueness of Pluto's gloom,
ribbed and torch-like, with their blaze of darkness spread
    blue
down flattening into points, flattened under the sweep of
    white day
torch-flower of the blue-smoking darkness, Pluto's dark-
    blue daze,
black lamps from the halls of Dis, burning dark blue,
giving off darkness, blue darkness, as Demeter's pale
    lamps give off light,
lead me then, lead the way.

Reach me a gentian, give me a torch!
let me guide myself with the blue, forked torch of this
    flower
down the darker and darker stairs, where blue is dark-
    ened on blueness
even where Persephone goes, just now, from the frosted
    September
to the sightless realm where darkness is awake upon the
    dark

and Persephone herself is but a voice
or a darkness invisible enfolded in the deeper dark
of the arms Plutonic, and pierced with the passion of
    dense gloom,
among the splendour of torches of darkness, shedding
    darkness on the lost bride and her groom.

THE WHITE HORSE

The youth walks up to the white horse, to put its halter
    on
and the horse looks at him in silence.
They are so silent they are in another world.

LITTLE FISH

The tiny fish enjoy themselves
in the sea.
Quick little splinters of life,
their little lives are fun to them
in the sea.

NOTHING TO SAVE

There is nothing to save, now all is lost,
but a tiny core of stillness in the heart
like the eye of a violet.

SNAKE

A snake came to my water-trough
On a hot, hot day, and I in pyjamas for the heat.
To drink there

In the deep, strange-scented shade of the great dark
    carob tree
I came down the steps with my pitcher
And must wait, must stand and wait, for there he was at
    the trough before me.

He reached down from a fissure in the earth-wall in the
    gloom
And trailed his yellow-brown slackness soft-bellied
    down, over the edge of the stone trough
And rested his throat upon the stone bottom,
And where the water had dripped from the tap, in a small
    clearness,
He sipped with his straight mouth,
Softly drank through his straight gums, into his slack
    long body.
Silently.

Someone was before me at my water-trough,
And I, like a second comer, waiting.

He lifted his head from his drinking, as cattle do,
And looked at me vaguely, as drinking cattle do,
And flickered his two-forked tongue from his lips, and
    mused a moment,
And stooped and drank a little more,
Being earth-brown, earth-golden from the burning bow-
    els of the earth
On the day of Sicilian July, with Etna smoking.

The voice of my education said to me
He must be killed,
For in Sicily the black, black snakes are innocent, the
    gold are venomous.

And voices in me said, If you were a man
You would take a stick and break him now, and finish him
    off.

But must I confess how I liked him,
How glad I was he had come like a guest in quiet, to drink
    at my water-trough
And depart peaceful, pacified, and thankless,
Into the burning bowels of this earth?

Was it cowardice, that I dared not kill him?
Was it perversity, that I longed to talk to him?
Was it humility, to feel so honoured?
I felt so honoured.

And yet those voices:
If you were not afraid, you would kill him!

And truly I was afraid, I was most afraid,
But even so, honoured still more
That he should seek my hospitality
From out the dark door of the secret earth.

He drank enough
And lifted his head, dreamily, as one who has drunken,
And flickered his tongue like a forked night on the air,
    so black,
Seeming to lick his lips,
And looked around like a god, unseeing, into the air,
And slowly turned his head,
And slowly, very slowly, as if thrice adream,
Proceeded to draw his slow length curving round
And climb again the broken bank of my wall-face.

And as he put his head into that dreadful hole,
And as he slowly drew up, snake-easing his shoulders,
    and entered farther,
A sort of horror, a sort of protest against his withdrawing
    into that horrid black hole,
Deliberately going into the blackness, and slowly draw-
    ing himself after,
Overcame me now his back was turned.

I looked around, I put down my pitcher.
I picked up a clumsy log
And threw it at the water-trough with a clatter.

I think I did not hit him,
But suddenly that part of him that was left behind con-
    vulsed in undignified haste,
Writhed like lightning, and was gone
Into the black hole, the earth-lipped fissure in the wall-
    front,

At which, in the intense still noon, I stared with fascina-
    tion.
And immediately I regretted it.
I thought how paltry, how vulgar, what a mean act!
I despised myself and the voices of my accursed human
    education.

And I thought of the albatross,
And I wished he would come back, my snake.

For he seemed to me again like a king,
Like a king in exile, uncrowned in the underworld,
Now due to be crowned again.

And so, I missed my chance with one of the lords
Of life.
And I have something to expiate;
A pettiness.

D. H. LAWRENCE

In his poetry D. H. Lawrence often writes as if the things he was looking at—birds, animals, trees, flowers—were clues to some great mystery of life, as if by being like them or following them or being lost in them he could have some kind of supreme experience, could be closer to what life is all about. That's the way he seems to think of the Bavarian gentians, the dark-blue flowers he feels lucky to have in his room. Have you felt—when you were reading, listening to music, or looking at something—that there was a mystery that you were just at the beginning of finding out about, and that what you were reading, hearing, or seeing was a special clue, meant perhaps, for you alone? That's something like what Lawrence is feeling. The gentians are so beautifully dark and blue that they seem to him like torches which can lead him somewhere else. He stares at their darkness and blueness and gets lost in them completely, as someone might get lost in listening to music. The dark-blue torches of the flowers lead him to Hades, a strange, dark, passionate realm which he is thrilled to be in. Hades for most people seems like a terrible place, but not for Lawrence. He finds a great beauty and truth there, a truth of darkness, freedom, passion, silence, earthiness, and aloneness. These are things he likes and talks of in so many of his poems and thinks that people need more of in their lives. The way people live now, Lawrence thinks, is mechanical, superficial, and dead. The book in which the gentians poem was first published was called *Birds, Beasts, and Flowers.* Other poems in it are, like "Bavarian Gentians," about the awareness of another world, which Lawrence gets from certain qualities of birds, beasts, and flowers —the royal grandeur of the snake, the quiet nobility of the white horse, the passionateness of the whale, the terrifying speed of the hummingbird, the merriment of little fish in the water.

Lawrence called his poems "acts of attention." Writing them, he seems to have concentrated on his subjects with enormous intensity, as if what he was looking at or thinking of and writing about were the only thing in the world. The snake becomes everything noble and grand; the gentians are all blueness and darkness, and they turn the whole world into a dark-blue kingdom. It is as though he were finding the truth—or, you could say, the power and excitement, the dark mystery (Lawrence's idea of truth wasn't a calm, quiet one)—that was hidden in these things.

Write a poem which, like Lawrence's, is an "act of attention." Write about a flower—yellow daffodils, white daisies, purple tulips, violets. Or someone's black or blond hair, or Christmas tree lights, or a sunrise, or the light of early evening, or just a color, such as red, green, or pink. Look at your subject or just think about it. Then let yourself get lost in it, as in music, as Lawrence seems to get lost in the gentians—in visions, in dreams. Let it be, as the gentians seem for Lawrence, the whole world for you while you write. Lawrence keeps repeating *dark* and *blue* in his poem as if the flowers were nothing but color, and as if that color were creating a new world, and as if saying the color again and again were part of what kept that world there. You may want to repeat the names of certain colors that way too. Your poem can be the story of a journey into the country or world of the color of that flower, a world which is visible only to you. Or let the flower or color be a torch, a sun, a flame, that leads you to another world. Try saying one thing that you find there, something you see or touch or feel, in every line.

Don't try to be reasonable. Your strangest ideas may be the best ones. What if, inside the orange, there were steps to the palace of the sun?

Ezra Pound
(1885–1972)

THE RIVER-MERCHANT'S
WIFE: A LETTER

While my hair was still cut straight across my forehead
I played about the front gate, pulling flowers.
You came by on bamboo stilts, playing horse,
You walked about my seat, playing with blue plums.
And we went on living in the village of Chōkan:
Two small people, without dislike or suspicion.

At fourteen I married My Lord you.
I never laughed, being bashful.
Lowering my head, I looked at the wall.
Called to, a thousand times, I never looked back.

At fifteen I stopped scowling,
I desired my dust to be mingled with yours
Forever and forever and forever.
Why should I climb the lookout?

At sixteen you departed,
You went into far Ku-tō-en, by the river of swirling ed-
    dies,

And you have been gone five months.
The monkeys make sorrowful noise overhead.

You dragged your feet when you went out.
By the gate now, the moss is grown, the different mosses,
Too deep to clear them away!
The leaves fall early this autumn, in wind.
The paired butterflies are already yellow with August
Over the grass in the West garden;
They hurt me. I grow older.
If you are coming down through the narrows of the river
    Kiang,
Please let me know beforehand,
And I will come out to meet you
        As far as Chō-fū-Sa.

    Li Po

SEPARATION ON
THE RIVER KIANG

Ko-jin goes west from Ko-kaku-ro,
The smoke-flowers are blurred over the river.
His lone sail blots the far sky.
And now I see only the river,
    The long Kiang, reaching heaven.

    Li Po

TAKING LEAVE OF A FRIEND

Blue mountains to the north of the walls,
White river winding about them;
Here we must make separation
And go out through a thousand miles of dead grass.

Mind like a floating wide cloud,
Sunset like the parting of old acquaintances
Who bow over their clasped hands at a distance.
Our horses neigh to each other
       as we are departing.

    Li Po

THE GARRET

Come, let us pity those who are better off than we are.
Come, my friend, and remember
       that the rich have butlers and no friends,
And we have friends and no butlers.
Come, let us pity the married and the unmarried.

Dawn enters with little feet
       like a gilded Pavlova,
And I am near my desire.
Nor has life in it aught better
Than this hour of clear coolness,
       the hour of waking together.

THE GARDEN

En robe de parade.—SAMAIN

Like a skein of loose silk blown against a wall
She walks by the railing of a path in Kensington Gardens,
And she is dying piece-meal
    of a sort of emotional anæmia.

And round about there is a rabble
Of the filthy, sturdy, unkillable infants of the very poor.
They shall inherit the earth.

In her is the end of breeding.
Her boredom is exquisite and excessive.
She would like some one to speak to her,
And is almost afraid that I
    will commit that indiscretion.

SESTINA: ALTAFORTE

LOQUITUR: *En* Bertrans de Born. Dante Alighieri put this
man in hell for that he was a stirrer up of strife. Eccovi!
Judge ye! Have I dug him up again? The scene is at his
castle, Altaforte. "Papiols" is his jongleur. "The Leopard,"
the *device* of Richard Cœur de Lion.

I

Damn it all! all this our South stinks peace.
You whoreson dog, Papiols, come! Let's to music!
I have no life save when the swords clash.

But ah! when I see the standards gold, vair, purple, op-
    posing
And the broad fields beneath them turn crimson,
Then howl I my heart nigh mad with rejoicing.

II

In hot summer have I great rejoicing
When the tempests kill the earth's foul peace,
And the lightnings from black heav'n flash crimson,
And the fierce thunders roar me their music
And the winds shriek through the clouds mad, opposing,
And through all the riven skies God's swords clash.

III

Hell grant soon we hear again the swords clash!
And the shrill neighs of destriers in battle rejoicing,
Spiked breast to spiked breast opposing!
Better one hour's stour than a year's peace
With fat boards, bawds, wine and frail music!
Bah! there's no wine like the blood's crimson!

IV

And I love to see the sun rise blood-crimson.
And I watch his spears through the dark clash
And it fills my heart with rejoicing
And pries wide my mouth with fast music
When I see him so scorn and defy peace,
His lone might 'gainst all darkness opposing.

V

The man who fears war and squats opposing
My words for stour, hath no blood of crimson
But is fit only to rot in womanish peace
Far from where worth's won and the swords clash
For the death of such sluts I go rejoicing;
Yea, I fill all the air with my music.

VI

Papiols, Papiols, to the music!
There's no sound like to swords swords opposing,
No cry like the battle's rejoicing
When our elbows and swords drip the crimson
And our charges 'gainst "The Leopard's" rush clash.
May God damn for ever all who cry "Peace!"

VII

And let the music of the swords make them crimson!
Hell grant soon we hear again the swords clash!
Hell blot black for alway the thought "Peace!"

ALBA

As cool as the pale wet leaves of lily of the valley
She lay beside me in the dawn.

EZRA POUND

Ezra Pound, who started publishing his work early in this century, had very strong ideas about what poetry should be like. Through his own poems and through what he wrote about poetry, he probably had more influence on English and American poets than any other modern writer. There were certain things that Pound didn't like about a lot of the poetry of the late nineteenth century and about the way people thought about and talked about poetry. He thought poetry should be strong and clear and truthful, should say things in as few words as possible, get straight to the point, and then stop, without flowery language, without moralizing or vagueness, without misty feelings. He didn't like the music made by regular meter and rhyme, but thought poetry should have a new music, plainer, less singsongy and less like a metronome. He saw something beautiful in the firmness and clarity of prose writing and thought poetry should have more of that quality. As for subject matter, he liked poetry that was about honest, plain feelings—love, desire, friendship, admiration, even hatred and aggression. Partly due to Pound's ideas and his poems, much poetry in English did become less flowery and less wordy; many poets gave up rhyme and meter; and more poets wrote more clearly. Yeats, Eliot, Williams, and many other poets were influenced by his work.

Pound found the qualities he liked in poems written in certain other cultures and at other times and in other languages. He translated many of these poems, doing his best to keep in his English version the qualities of the original one. He thought it was just about as important to make a really good new translation of a great poem, one that was idiomatic and natural and clear, as it was to write a new poem. Pound translated Chinese poetry,

Latin poetry, Provençal poetry (Provence is a part of southern France, which up until the thirteenth century had its own language and culture), and Japanese poetic plays. He also translated poems from German, French, Italian, Greek, and Anglo-Saxon. His translations are an important part of his work. Pound felt not only that translating brought works back to life, but also that it was good preparation for a poet's own writing. His translations were also a way of showing people what poetry should be like.

"The River-Merchant's Wife: A Letter" is a translation of a poem by the great Chinese poet Li Po. The poem is about love, but it says nothing about love directly. The young wife's restraint makes it even clearer that her love is deep and certain. It is unnecessary to explain your feelings when they are simple and strong and sure. She talks in the simple, tender way that people talk to each other when very much between them is already understood. She makes no reproach, no demand. She doesn't even ask him to come back. She just says, "If you are coming down through the narrows . . ." When she was with him, time passed, she changed, and she learned to love him deeply. Now time is passing again, she is changing again, but he isn't there. When she sees all around her the way time is passing, it hurts her, she feels in it his absence. She will make the time shorter, even if only by a little, by coming out to meet him on his way back. "The River-Merchant's Wife: A Letter" is very different from the kind of exaggerated, overelaborate romantic love poetry that Pound so much disliked.

Write a poem which, like this one, is a letter. The person you write it to doesn't actually have to be far away. Write it, perhaps, to a good friend, or to someone you know very little but have thought about, or to someone you imagine, or maybe to someone that you don't know if you'll ever see again. It can even be to someone who is dead. You might try organizing the poem in somewhat the way this one is; that is, in each stanza you could talk about a different time in your life, a different age. It might be helpful to think of a certain day you remember very strongly when you were that age. Where exactly were you? And what were you doing, what did you wear, what was your hair like then? Was the person you are writing the letter to there? Instead of talking about your emotions, see if you can suggest them by talking about what you said or saw or did. In the last part of the poem, talk about what is happening to you now. Again, talk more about the weather, and the way everything looks, and what you are doing than about what you feel. Maybe the last stanza could, as in Pound's poem, contain a wish. This poem doesn't begin with "Dear" or end with "Love," but you can begin and end your poem that way if you like. Or you can show that it's a letter only by its title.

T. S. Eliot
(1888 –1965)

THE LOVE SONG OF
J. ALFRED PRUFROCK

S'io credesse che mia risposta fosse
A persona che mai tornasse al mondo,
Questa fiamma staria senza piu scosse.
Ma perciocche giammai di questo fondo
Non torno vivo alcun, s'i'odo il vero,
Senza tema d'infamia ti rispondo. [1]

Let us go then, you and I,
When the evening is spread out against the sky
Like a patient etherised upon a table;
Let us go, through certain half-deserted streets,
The muttering retreats
Of restless nights in one-night cheap hotels
And sawdust restaurants with oyster-shells:
Streets that follow like a tedious argument
Of insidious intent
To lead you to an overwhelming question . . .

---

[1] "If I thought I replied to one who might go back to the world, this flame should never move. But since—if what I hear be true— no one has ever returned from this gulf alive, I answer without fear of infamy."

Oh, do not ask, "What is it?"
Let us go and make our visit.

In the room the women come and go
Talking of Michelangelo.

The yellow fog that rubs its back upon the windowpanes,
The yellow smoke that rubs its muzzle on the window-
     panes
Licked its tongue into the corners of the evening,
Lingered upon the pools that stand in drains,
Let fall upon its back the soot that falls from chimneys,
Slipped by the terrace, made a sudden leap,
And seeing that it was a soft October night,
Curled once about the house, and fell asleep.

And indeed there will be time
For the yellow smoke that slides along the street,
Rubbing its back upon the window-panes;
There will be time, there will be time
To prepare a face to meet the faces that you meet;
There will be time to murder and create,
And time for all the works and days of hands
That lift and drop a question on your plate;
Time for you and time for me,
And time yet for a hundred indecisions,
And for a hundred visions and revisions,
Before the taking of a toast and tea.

In the room the women come and go
Talking of Michelangelo.

And indeed there will be time
To wonder, "Do I dare?" and, "Do I dare?"
Time to turn back and descend the stair,
With a bald spot in the middle of my hair—

(They will say: "How his hair is growing thin!")
My morning coat, my collar mounting firmly to the chin,
My necktie rich and modest, but asserted by a simple
    pin—
(They will say: "But how his arms and legs are thin!")
Do I dare
Disturb the universe?
In a minute there is time
For decisions and revisions which a minute will reverse.

For I have known them all already, known them all:
Have known the evenings, mornings, afternoons,
I have measured out my life with coffee spoons;
I know the voices dying with a dying fall
Beneath the music from a farther room.
      So how should I presume?

And I have known the eyes already, known them all—
The eyes that fix you in a formulated phrase,
And when I am formulated, sprawling on a pin,
When I am pinned and wriggling on the wall,
Then how should I begin
To spit out all the butt-ends of my days and ways?
      And how should I presume?

And I have known the arms already, known them all—
Arms that are braceleted and white and bare
(But in the lamplight, downed with light brown hair!)
Is it perfume from a dress
That makes me so digress?
Arms that lie along a table, or wrap about a shawl.
      And should I then presume?
      And how should I begin?
            . . .

Shall I say, I have gone at dusk through narrow streets
And watched the smoke that rises from the pipes
Of lonely men in shirt-sleeves, leaning out of win-
  dows?. . .

I should have been a pair of ragged claws
Scuttling across the floors of silent seas.

                    . . .

And the afternoon, the evening, sleeps so peacefully!
Smoothed by long fingers,
Asleep . . . tired . . . or it malingers,
Stretched on the floor, here beside you and me.
Should I, after tea and cakes and ices,
Have the strength to force the moment to its crisis?
But though I have wept and fasted, wept and prayed,
Though I have seen my head (grown slightly bald)
  brought in upon a platter,
I am no prophet—and here's no great matter;
I have seen the moment of my greatness flicker,
And I have seen the eternal Footman hold my coat, and
  snicker,
And in short, I was afraid.

And would it have been worth it, after all,
After the cups, the marmalade, the tea,
Among the porcelain, among some talk of you and me,
Would it have been worth while,
To have bitten off the matter with a smile,
To have squeezed the universe into a ball,
To roll it toward some overwhelming question,
To say: "I am Lazarus, come from the dead,
Come back to tell you all, I shall tell you all"—
If one, settling a pillow by her head,
    Should say: "That is not what I meant at all.
    That is not it, at all."

And would it have been worth it, after all,
Would it have been worth while,
After the sunsets and the dooryards and the sprinkled
    streets,
After the novels, after the teacups, after the skirts that
    trail along the floor—
And this, and so much more?—
It is impossible to say just what I mean!
But as if a magic lantern threw the nerves in patterns on
    a screen:
Would it have been worth while
If one, settling a pillow or throwing off a shawl,
And turning toward the window, should say:
    "That is not it at all,
    That is not what I meant, at all."

· · ·

No! I am not Prince Hamlet, nor was meant to be;
Am an attendant lord, one that will do
To swell a progress, start a scene or two,
Advise the prince; no doubt, an easy tool,
Deferential, glad to be of use,
Politic, cautious, and meticulous;
Full of high sentence, but a bit obtuse;
At times, indeed, almost ridiculous—
Almost, at times, the Fool.

I grow old . . . I grow old . . .
I shall wear the bottoms of my trousers rolled.

Shall I part my hair behind? Do I dare to eat a peach?
I shall wear white flannel trousers, and walk upon the
    beach.
I have heard the mermaids singing, each to each.

I do not think that they will sing to me.

I have seen them riding seaward on the waves
Combing the white hair of the waves blown back
When the wind blows the water white and black.

We have lingered in the chambers of the sea
By sea-girls wreathed with seaweed red and brown
Till human voices wake us, and we drown.

PRELUDES

I

The winter evening settles down
With smell of steaks in passageways.
Six o'clock.
The burnt-out ends of smoky days.
And now a gusty shower wraps
The grimy scraps
Of withered leaves about your feet
And newspapers from vacant lots;
The showers beat
On broken blinds and chimney-pots,
And at the corner of the street
A lonely cab-horse steams and stamps.
And then the lighting of the lamps.

II

The morning comes to consciousness
Of faint stale smells of beer
From the sawdust-trampled street
With all its muddy feet that press
To early coffee-stands.
With the other masquerades

That time resumes,
One thinks of all the hands
That are raising dingy shades
In a thousand furnished rooms.

III

You tossed a blanket from the bed,
You lay upon your back, and waited;
You dozed, and watched the night revealing
The thousand sordid images
Of which your soul was constituted;
They flickered against the ceiling.
And when all the world came back
And the light crept up between the shutters
And you heard the sparrows in the gutters,
You had such a vision of the street
As the street hardly understands;
Sitting along the bed's edge, where
You curled the papers from your hair,
Or clasped the yellow soles of feet
In the palms of both soiled hands.

IV

His soul stretched tight across the skies
That fade behind a city block,
Or trampled by insistent feet
At four and five and six o'clock;
And short square fingers stuffing pipes,
And evening newspapers, and eyes
Assured of certain certainties,
The conscience of a blackened street
Impatient to assume the world.

I am moved by fancies that are curled
Around these images, and cling:
The notion of some infinitely gentle

Infinitely suffering thing.
Wipe your hand across your mouth, and laugh;
The worlds revolve like ancient women
Gathering fuel in vacant lots.

T. S. ELIOT

T. S. Eliot, from the 1920's to the 1950's, was thought by many people to be the poet who had best captured in his poetry the spirit of the modern world—that is to say, the condition of people's minds, feelings, and lives in America and Western Europe. The condition he finds is despair; the mood in his poems is anxiety, fatigue, hopelessness, a feeling of meaninglessness, weakness, depression, an inability to act. In Eliot's early poems, such as "Prufrock," "The Preludes," and *The Waste Land,* the suffering has no clearly known cause and there seems to be no answer.

One thing that made this poetry seem so serious and important was Eliot's way of confronting in his poetry the whole "real" world of his time, the world that newspapers and historians and sociologists write about. His poems have a way of taking it—the outside world of society, culture, politics—very personally, the way you would have to take it personally if the air were being poisoned and everything you did or tried to do were affected by that; if you couldn't breathe or speak or drink a glass of water without its affecting you; if you couldn't ignore it or escape it or overcome it or even understand it.

Prufrock and, in other poems, other characters—all those in *The Waste Land,* for example—are victims of the modern world, and they all show what is so awful about it. They are useless, unable to act, unable to love; they've been living in a poisoned civilization too long and have no chance to be happy, to change what is happening to them, or to change themselves. These characters are a new kind of hero or main character for poetry to have. They are not valiant and adventurous; they are not even healthy or competent or determined. Prufrock is unable to do anything except continue to go to tea parties, which make him feel miserable. Inside himself he feels romantic and poetic and sensitive—his great ambition is to be able to talk to a woman and tell her what he feels. But he can't do it. He's afraid she'd make fun of him, that she'd say, "That is not what I meant at all." He feels helpless. He keeps saying and thinking and doing and hearing the same things over and over again. He feels frozen, petrified in the social setting he is in. But he knows that nothing is going to change, except that he'll grow old and seem even more ridiculous. The only time he feels easy and sensuous and happy, as he suggests at the end of the poem, is when he's asleep or perhaps daydreaming, imagining he's with mermaids. Then reality in the form of human voices wakes him up, and he is "dead" again.

The poem is not an objective description of Prufrock's life. Prufrock himself is talking. This kind of poem is called a *dramatic monologue*—that is, a character, not the author, is speaking, as if from a stage. It is not, of course, the way anyone talks to anyone but a kind of thinking out loud. Prufrock wouldn't be very interesting if he were just some kind of symbol of what's wrong with the modern world. He seems a real person with real and recognizable feelings.

It is not hard to sympathize with Prufock. Almost everyone has known people who seem to live empty, meaningless lives. And almost everyone, at one time or another, has felt himself to be helpless in some kind of social trap. It is easy to become confused, to become so involved with what you are supposed to do, with what you're expected to do, with what other people are counting on you to do, that after a while you feel that your life has nothing to do with you. At such times people often feel detached from what they wanted, from who they really are, from what their own ideas and hopes are. Or they feel that life itself is shallow and purposeless and without value. Or perhaps they feel split in two—with the real self suffering and full of secret longings, while the superficial self continues to go through the motions, afraid to try to challenge anything, to try to change anything. Fortunately, for most people these feelings don't last long, since most people, unlike Prufrock, can change the situation they are in. But when you feel like this, it is common to feel, as Prufock does, that the situation is hopeless and endless.

Write a dramatic monologue in which the hero is someone who is something like Prufrock. The hero can be yourself or a part of yourself, or it can be someone you know or have known. You may want to give the character a name. Let the character think out loud, as Prufrock does, talking on the one hand about what he feels and wants and thinks, and on the other hand about what he actually does and says and hears. These things can be mixed together in a sort of rambling, disorganized way, with, as in "Prufrock," a kind of repetitiveness. In "Prufrock," what people say and do and think and wear and so on seems always the same. Nothing changes; nothing is new. The women are always coming and going, talking of Michelangelo; there are the repetitions of "How should I presume?" and "There will be time." In your own poem, try using a lot of repetition—repetitions of polite phrases, of thoughts, of actions, of scenes. You could, as Eliot does in "Prufrock," begin various sections with phrases like "I have known" or "I have seen" or "Would it have been worth it?" Don't philosophize or generalize about what is wrong. Rather, be in the middle of it—with the rooms, furniture, yards, sidewalks, clothes, dinners, stores, books. One way Eliot creates a feeling of emptiness is with a somewhat singsongy and dead-sounding music and with dreary rhymes: *afternoons* rhymes with *coffee spoons*, *room* with *presume*. Reading Eliot's poetry aloud is a good way to catch on to this poetic music, after which you may want to try using it in your own poem.

Vladimir Mayakowsky
(1893–1930)

From *"A Cloud in Trousers"*

PROLOGUE

Your thoughts,
dreaming in a softened brain
like a stuffed lackey on a greasy couch,
I will tease with a blood-soaked scrap of heart
and satiate my impudent, caustic contempt.

There is not a single gray hair in my soul,
there is no grandfatherly gentleness!
Shaking the world with the might of my voice,
I go by—a handsome
twentytwoyearold.

Dear ones!
You play love on a violin.
The crude play love on a drum.
But unlike me, you can't turn yourselves inside out
and become entirely lips.

Out of your cambric drawing rooms,
come and learn,
officious officials of the angelic league.

And you who calmly thumb through your lips
the way a cook flips the pages of a cookbook.

If you want—
I'll rage on raw meat
—or, changing tones like the sky—
if you want—
I'll be irreproachably gentle,
not a man, but a cloud in trousers.

I do not believe there is a blossomy Nice!
Again I glorify
men as stale as sickrooms
and women as battered as proverbs.

I

You think malaria makes me rave?

It happened.
In Odessa it happened.

"I'll come at four," Maria said.

Eight.
Nine.
Ten.

The evening
fled from the window
into the terror of the night,
leering,
Decemberish.

At my decrepit back
the candelabras cackled and sniggered.

You won't recognize me now:
a sinewy hulk,
groaning,
writhing.
What can such a huge clod want?
A huge clod can want so much!

Is it really important
whether we are cast in bronze
or whether the heart is a cold piece of iron?
At night I want to hide my clanging
in softness,
in woman.

And so,
massive,
hunched up at the window,
I melt the glass with my forehead.
Will there be love?
And what kind—
a big love or a crumb of love?
How could such a small body have a big one:
it must be a small,
humble love
which shies from the honking of cars
and prefers the bells of horse-trams.

More and more,
nuzzling the rain
my face against its pockmarked face,
I wait,
splashed by the thundering surf of the city.

Midnight, running loose with a knife,
caught up,
slashed—

get away!
Twelve o'clock fell
like a head from the chopping block.

Gray raindrops on the windowpanes
screamed together,
amassing a mask,
as though the gargoyles
of Notre Dame were howling.

Damn you!
Isn't it enough?
Soon screams will rip my mouth apart.

I hear,
quietly,
a nerve jump up
like a sick man from his bed.
Barely, barely moving
at first,
it soon skittered about,
agitated,
distinct.
Two more joined it
failing madly in a desperate dance.

The plaster crashed on the floor below.

Nerves—
big,
little,
thousands of nerves!—
galloped crazily
until
their legs gave out!

But through the room, night oozed and oozed—
a heavy eye could not get out of the bog.

Suddenly the doors rattled,
as if the teeth of the hotel
were chattering.

You came in,
abrupt, like "take it or leave it!"
Maiming your suede gloves,
you said,
"Y'know,
I'm getting married."

So what.
Get married.
It's nothing.
I can take it.
See how calm I am!
Like the pulse
of a corpse.

Remember?
You used to say:
"Jack London,
money,
love,
passion."
But I saw only one thing:
You were a Gioconda
which had to be stolen!

And they stole you.

With the arch of my brows flaming,
I will gamble again in love.

What of it!
Homeless hobos sometimes find
shelter in burnt-out houses!

Are you teasing?
"You have fewer emeralds of insanity
than a beggar has kopecks!"
Remember!
Pompeii perished
when they teased Vesuvius!

Hey!
Gentlemen!
Amateurs
of sacrilege,
crime,
carnage—
have you seen
the terror of terrors—
my face
when
I
am absolutely calm?

I feel
my "I"
is too small.
Someone stubbornly bursts out of me.

Hello!
Who's speaking?
Mamma?
Mamma!
Your son is gloriously sick!
His heart is on fire.

Tell his sisters, Lyuda and Olya,
he has nowhere to hide.

Every word,
every joke
he vomits from his sizzling mouth,
jumps like a naked prostitute
from a burning brothel.

People sniff—
burnt flesh!
A brigade drives up,
shining,
in helmets!
No hobnail boots here, please!
Tell the firemen:
climb a burning heart with gentleness.
I'll do it myself.
I'll pump barrels from tearful eyes.
Brace myself against the ribs.
I'll jump! I'll jump! I'll jump!
Everything has collapsed.
You can't jump out of the heart.

From cracks of lips
a charred kiss throws itself
on a smoldering face.

Mamma!
I can't sing.
In the chapel of the heart
the choir loft catches fire!

Scorched figurines of words and numbers
scramble from the brain

like children from a burning building.
So fear
stretched out
flaming arms on the *Lusitania*
to clutch for the sky.
Shaking people,
a hundred-eyed blaze bursts
from the docks
into the quiet of the apartment,
Shriek
into the centuries,
if you can, one last cry: I am on fire!

   2
Praise me!
The great are nothing to me.
On every achievement
I stamp "NIHIL."

I never want
to read anything.
Book?
What are books!

    . . .

   4
Maria! Maria! Maria!
Let me in, Maria!
I can't stay out on the streets!
Don't you want to?
Will you wait
until my cheeks cave in,
sampled by everyone,
then I'll come,
stale,

toothlessly muttering
that today I am
"remarkably honest!"

Maria,
you see—
my shoulders are already drooping.

In the streets
people will poke holes in the fat of four-story goiters,
thrust out their small eyes,
sickly from forty years of dragging about,
to snicker
at my having between my teeth
—again—
the stale crust of yesterday's caress.

The rain sobbed all over the sidewalks;
the scoundrel, condensed into puddles,
all wet, licks the cobblestone-beaten corpse of streets.
And on his gray eyelashes—
yes!—
tears flow from the eyes—
yes!—
on his icicle eyelashes
from the sagging eyes of drainpipes.

The snout of the rain drooled on all the pedestrians,
but flabby athlete after athlete flashed by in carriages:
stuffed to the eyeballs,
they burst,
grease dribbled through the cracks,
and together with chewed-over rolls
and the cud of old ground meat
it flowed down in a turbid river from the carriages.

Maria!
How can you cram a gentle word into a fat ear?
A bird
begs with songs,
and sings,
hungry and resonant.
But I am a man, Maria,
a simple man,
coughed up by consumptive night into the dirty hand of
the Presyana.

Maria, d'you want such a man?
Let me in, Maria!
With convulsive fingers I'll grab the iron throat of the
doorbell!

Maria!

The street-pastures have gone wild.
On my neck are the scratches of the mob.

Open up!

I'm hurt!

You see—ladies' hatpins
Are stuck into my eyes!

You've let me in.

Darling,
don't be afraid
if sweat-bellied women, like a wet mountain,
sit on my bovine shoulders—
so through life I drag
millions of huge true loves

and a million million vile little loves.
Don't be afraid
if once again,
in the storminess of infidelity,
I cling to thousands of pretty faces—
"admirers of Mayakowsky!"—
this is really the dynasty
of queens ascending the heart of a madman.

Maria, come closer!

Whether in naked shame
or shaking in fear,
just give me the unwithered charm of your lips:
my heart and I have not once lived as long as May,
and in my past life
there are only a hundred Aprils.

Maria!
The poet sings sonnets to Tiana,
but I—
all flesh,
all man—
I simply ask for your body
as a Christian asks:
"Give us this day
our daily bread!"

Maria—give!

Maria!
I am afraid of forgetting your name
as a poet is afraid of forgetting
some word
born in the tortures of nights,
great as god himself.

I will love and cherish
your body
the way an unwanted
friendless
soldier,
war amputee,
cherishes his only remaining leg.

Maria!
Don't you want me?
You don't want me!
Don't you—

Ha!

It means—again
I will take my heart,
spattered by tears,
and carry it
like a dog
carries
a paw run over by a train
back to its kennel.

With the blood of my heart I make the road happy,
it sticks like flowers to a dusty tunic.
A thousand times the sun will dance,
like Salome, around the earth,
the head of the Baptist.

And when my collection of years
has danced to the end—
a million bloodstains will be strewn
on the path to my father's house.

. . .

Winged swindlers!
Cower in heaven!
Ruffle your feathers in frightened shaking!
You, reeking of incense, I'll rip open
from here to Alaska!

Let me in!

You can't stop me.
I may be lying,
or I may be telling the truth,
but I couldn't be any calmer.
You see—
they've beheaded the stars
and bloodied the sky with carnage!

Hey, you!
Heaven!
Off with your hat!
I'm coming!

Quiet.

The universe sleeps,
a huge star-infested ear
resting on a paw.

translated by Peter Bogdanoff

VLADIMIR MAYAKOWSKY

The Russian poet Vladimir Mayakowsky wrote "A Cloud in Trousers" when he was twenty-two—as he says rather boastfully in his poem, "a handsome/twentytwoyear-old." The story in the poem is that the poet loves Maria, and he's dying to see her. She finally comes to him (very, very late) and says she's going to marry someone else. Who wouldn't be angry? But for Mayakowsky, being upset is like a storm, a volcano erupting, an earthquake. His feelings seem very strong to him, so strong that it seems he can't contain them, can't bear them. He says, "My 'I' is too small for me." By his "I" he means his regular self. His other, poetic, emotional self feels enormous, boundless, and everything that happens to him seems like a tremendous event. He feels he's caught fire, like part of a city: "A hundred-eyed blaze bursts/from the docks/into the quiet of the apartment . . . I am on fire!" His body is like a building in which thousands of things are happening, all of which he is intensely aware of: he feels "a nerve jump up/like a sick man from his bed." And everything that is happening around him seems just as animated and as violent as what is in his feelings. The clouds are like "white workers breaking up/after declaring a violent strike against the sky"; doors rattle "as if the teeth of the hotel/were chattering"; midnight runs loose with a knife. Even his rare calm feelings are extravagant—he says he can be "irreproachably gentle . . . like a cloud in trousers."

Mayakowsky protests, makes announcements, begins the story, then stops and yells. He gets angry again; he makes threats; he talks to the angels, to God; he picks up the telephone in the middle of the poem and starts making emergency phone calls: "Hello! Who's speaking? Mamma? Mamma! Your son is gloriously sick!" His loss of Maria isn't the only thing that is wrong; it makes it clear to him what is wrong everywhere—with Russia, with society, with poetry. He is furious at old-fashioned love poets (it's such poets he's shouting at when the poem begins). They, he says, don't know what love is. They don't know what poetry is, either. Poetry is painful, tough, and modern. It isn't pretty and elegant and sweetly flowing. It's about hospitals, streetcars, and hotels, not about nightingales and roses. His poem, he feels, has the real truth in it—it is huge and crazy and tough and enraged.

Probably everyone has, at one time or another, had feelings that were terribly powerful, that seemed too big to be borne, too strong to be kept inside—feelings of love, of loneliness, of anger, of terror. In regular life we learn to control our emotions, to "contain" ourselves, to be reasonable and quiet and objective. Strong emotions can be good for poetry, though. Emotion can put music into language. And losing control, in poetry, can be good for inspiration.

Try writing a poem of rage or protest. It could be about something that you are, in fact, really furious about—a fight with a friend, for instance, or some way you have been treated that is wrong or unfair. Or you can exaggerate or invent feelings about some rather ordinary injustices—that you have to do what other people say, that the weather is horrible, that you are a certain age or live in a certain place. Let yourself go, as Mayakowsky does. Don't try to be modest and fair and objective. Be wild and crazy and boastful. Exaggerate everything. Assume that what happened to you is the worst possible disaster, as important as anything that could happen to cities, countries, mountains, or the ocean. Try comparing your feelings or parts of your body (your heart, your brain, your eyes) to parts of a collapsing, besieged, or disease-ridden city. Make your poem full of streets, hotels, subways, factories, bridges, airports, smokestacks, and electricity. You might like to make an emergency phone call in the middle of the poem—to your mother, to a friend. Talk from the midst of what you are feeling as if it were all still happening. Be unreasonable, if you want to, bringing in whatever injustices or feelings that, for the moment, seem related. Use tough words—not obscenity, but the kind Mayakowsky uses: words like *amputee*, *swindlers*, *reeking*. Use short lines, or some short ones and some long ones. The poem can change around a lot—maybe sometimes it will be loud like a scream, sometimes quiet like a whisper.

E. E. Cummings
(1894 – 1962)

SPRING IS LIKE A PERHAPS HAND

Spring is like a perhaps hand
(which comes carefully
out of Nowhere)arranging
a window,into which people look(while
people stare
arranging and changing placing
carefully there a strange
thing and a known thing here)and

changing everything carefully

spring is like a perhaps
Hand in a window
(carefully to
and fro moving New and
Old things,while
people stare carefully
moving a perhaps
fraction of flower here placing
an inch of air there)and

without breaking anything.

MY SWEET OLD ETCETERA

my sweet old etcetera
aunt lucy during the recent

war could and what
is more did tell you just
what everybody was fighting

for,
my sister

isabel created hundreds
(and
hundreds)of socks not to
mention shirts fleaproof earwarmers

etcetera wristers etcetera, my
mother hoped that

i would die etcetera
bravely of course my father used
to become hoarse talking about how it was
a privilege and if only he
could meanwhile my

self etcetera lay quietly
in the deep mud et

cetera
(dreaming,
et
      cetera, of
Your smile
eyes knees and of your Etcetera)

PARIS; THIS APRIL SUNSET COMPLETELY UTTERS

Paris; this April sunset completely utters
utters serenely silently a cathedral

before whose upward lean magnificent face
the streets turn young with rain,

spiral acres of bloated rose
coiled within cobalt miles of sky
yield to and heed
the mauve
           of twilight(who slenderly descends,
daintily carrying in her eyes the dangerous first stars)
people move love hurry in a gently

arriving gloom and
see!(the new moon
fills abruptly with sudden silver
these torn pockets of lame and begging colour)while
there and here the lithe indolent prostitute
Night, argues

with certain houses

SOMEWHERE I HAVE NEVER TRAVELLED,GLADLY BEYOND

somewhere i have never travelled,gladly beyond
any experience,your eyes have their silence:
in your most frail gesture are things which enclose me,
or which i cannot touch because they are too near

your slightest look easily will unclose me
though i have closed myself as fingers,
you open always petal by petal myself as Spring opens
(touching skilfully,mysteriously)her first rose

or if your wish be to close me,i and
my life will shut very beautifully,suddenly,
as when the heart of this flower imagines
the snow carefully everywhere descending;

nothing which we are to perceive in this world equals
the power of your intense fragility:whose texture
compels me with the colour of its countries,
rendering death and forever with each breathing

(i do not know what it is about you that closes
and opens;only something in me understands
the voice of your eyes is deeper than all roses)
nobody,not even the rain,has such small hands

E. E. CUMMINGS

Modern poetry in general is sometimes described as "experimental." That is because modern poets have felt free to try new ways of putting words together in order to find a way of writing in which they could say what they wanted to say. In the work of E. E. Cummings, though, almost every poem seems like some kind of experiment, like another investigation into the use of words. His poetry constantly breaks all the rules. Adverbs are used as adjectives, adjectives as nouns, lines don't begin with capitals, punctuation is left out or used in an eccentric way. He begins in the middle of a sentence, sentences are left unfinished, words are invented, lines are very short or very long for no apparent reason, capital letters and blank spaces appear in peculiar places, poems are given numbers instead of titles.

Somewhat surprisingly, Cummings's poems are fairly easy to understand. The effect of this experimentation is not to take the meaning away but to add or emphasize a certain kind of meaning. His way of writing seems to call attention to the sense of each word, so that each word counts and is important in the poem. For instance, in "Spring Is Like a Perhaps Hand," *perhaps* and *carefully*—adverbs that are often lost in a regular sentence—are placed so unexpectedly that they become as important as more visually vivid words, such as *flower* and *window.* The capitalization of *Nowhere* and *New* and *Old* has a similar effect. It makes these words important in a new way. And the irregular use of parentheses gives a new kind of life and suggestiveness to them. In "My Sweet Old Etcetera," *etcetera,* which hardly ever means anything at all, is placed so that it suggests a great deal, and something slightly different each time it is used.

Experimenting with words this way is a little like a

game. One effect of so many surprises in a poem may be a tone that you aren't used to in serious poetry, one that is light, changeable, and funny. But playing with words can be a good and serious way to discover how to use words to say certain things you couldn't otherwise say.

A good way to begin experimenting with words is to start with something that is already written—one of your poems or a paragraph from a newspaper or a novel. Then change everything around. Try everything you can think of with words, parts of speech, commas, quotes, parentheses, strange spellings, capitals, small letters, spaces, short lines, word divisions, just to see what happens. Keep changing everything around until it has a different sense and sound from what you began with and is something that pleases or amuses you in some way or another.

Or try writing a poem that's a description of someone or something—not necessarily a realistic description, but a description inspried by what the subject makes you think of or feel. Write about a season, the snow, the beach, the recess grounds of a school, someone you like or love. Try beginning the poem in the middle of a sentence. Use the words in ways that surprise you. Think about every word. Let the punctuation surprise you too. Try putting in words that seem to have nothing to do with the description; see if there's a place you can make them fit. It doesn't really matter if you end up with a different subject from the one you began with. This is one way to let the materials of poetry inspire you and help you to write a poem.

Federico García Lorca
(1899–1936)

THE MOON RISES

When the moon comes up
the bells are lost
and there appear
impenetrable paths.

When the moon comes up
the sea blankets the earth
and the heart feels
like an island in infinity.

No one eats oranges
under the full moon.
One must eat
cold green fruit.

When the moon comes up
with a hundred equal faces,
silver money
sobs in the pocket.

translated by William B. Logan

BALLAD OF LUNA, LUNA

The moon came to the forge
with her petticoat of spikenard.
The boy looks and looks at her.
The boy is looking at her.
In the whirling air
the moon moves her arms
and shows off, slick and pure,
her breasts of hard tin.
—Run luna, luna, luna.
If the gypsies should come
they'd make of your heart
necklaces and white rings.
—Child, let me dance.
When the gypsies come
they'll find you over the anvil
with your eyelids closed.
—Run luna, luna, luna,
for now I can hear their horses.
—Child, let me alone. Don't stamp
on my starched whiteness.

The rider came closer,
playing on the drum of the plain.
Inside the forge, the boy
has his eyes closed.

Through the olive grove,
bronze and dreaming, came the gypsies.
Their heads upraised
and their eyes half-closed.

How the tawny owl sings,
oh, how it sings in the tree!
Through the sky goes the moon
with a boy by the hand.

Inside the forge the gypsies
cry, letting out shrieks.
The wind is watching, watching it.
The wind is watching over it.

translated by William B. Logan

LITTLE VIENNESE WALTZ

In Vienna there are ten young girls,
a shoulder on which death is sobbing,
and a forest of stuffed doves.
There's a fragment of the morning
in the frost's museum.
There's a salon with a thousand windows.
      Ay, ay, ay, ay!
Take this waltz with your mouth shut.

    This waltz, this waltz, this waltz,
of itself and of cognac and death,
that dips its gown's tail in the sea.

    I love you, I love you, I love you,
with the dead book and the easy chair,
down the melancholy hallway,
in the lily's dark loft,

in our own bed of the moon,
and in the dance the tortoise dreams.
      Ay, ay, ay, ay!
Take this waltz bent at the waist.

    There are in Vienna four mirrors
where your mouth and the echos play.
There's a death for pianoforte
that paints the young boys blue.
There are beggars on the rooftops.
There are fresh bouquets of cries.
      Ay, ay, ay, ay!
Take this waltz which is dying in my arms.

    Because I love you, my love, I love you
in the loft where the children play,
dreaming of the old lights of Hungary
through the noises of the weak afternoon,
watching the sheep and the lilies of snow
on the dark silence of your brow.
      Ay, ay, ay, ay!
Take this "I'll love you forever" of a waltz.

    In Vienna I'll dance with you
in a costume with
a river's head.
Look what hyacinth banks I have!
I'll leave my mouth between your legs,
my soul in white lilies and photographs,
and in the dark waves of your walking
I want, my love, my love, to leave,
violin and sepulcher, the ribbons of the waltz.

translated by William B. Logan

DAWN

Dawn in New York comes
with four columns of slime
and a hurricane of doves
splattering in the stagnant water.

Dawn in New York wails
on the huge stairways
searching among the angles
for spikenards of haggard pain.

Dawn comes and no one takes her in his mouth
because there there's no chance of morning or hope.
Sometimes the coins in mad swarms
slam into and devour abandoned children.

The first to come out know in their bones
that there will be no paradise, no lovers stripped of
        leaves;
they know they're going to the slime of numbers and
        laws,
to the games without art, to the sweats without issue.

The light is buried by chains and noise
shamelessly defying a science with no roots.
There are people staggering through the suburbs unable
        to sleep
as if they'd just escaped a shipwreck of blood.

translated by William B. Logan

SONG OF BLACK CUBANS

When the full moon rises
I'll go to Santiago de Cuba.
I'll go to Santiago
in a black water car.
I'll go to Santiago.
The palm leaf roofs will sing.
I'll go to Santiago.
When the palm tree wants to be a stork.
I'll go to Santiago.
And the banana tree a jellyfish.
I'll go to Santiago.
With Fonseca's blond head.
I'll go to Santiago.
And Romeo and Juliet's rose.
I'll go to Santiago.
Paper sea and coin silver.
I'll go to Santiago.
Oh Cuba, oh rhythm of dry seeds!
I'll go to Santiago.
Oh hot waist and drop of wood!
I'll go to Santiago.
Harp of living tree trunks, cayman, tobacco flower!
I'll go to Santiago.
I always said I'd go to Santiago
in a black water car.
I'll go to Santiago.
Alcohol and breeze in the wheels.
I'll go to Santiago.
My coral in the darkness.
I'll go to Santiago.
The sea drowned in the sand.
I'll go to Santiago.
White heat, dead fruit.

I'll go to Santiago.
Oh bovine freshness of reeds!
Oh Cuba! Oh curve of sighs and clay!
I'll go to Santiago.

translated by William B. Logan

FEDERICO GARCÍA LORCA

The Spanish poet Federico García Lorca spent some time in New York and in Cuba when he was in his early thirties. In 1936, when he was thirty-eight, Lorca was killed by the Fascists during the Spanish Civil War. His early poems, written in Andalusia, where he was born, are often like strange folk tales or fairy tales—sometimes stories about nature, sometimes about the lives of the gypsies. The poems written in New York are rougher and freer and less songlike and have other subjects.

Lorca's poetry is always wild and strange in one way or another. There are mysterious places and unexplainable things and extraordinary events. There is a forest of stuffed doves, a salon with a thousand windows, a paper sea, a black water car. Money "sobs in the pocket," the New York dawn has "four columns of slime," the "palm tree wants to be a stork." Lorca's way of writing makes everything he writes about seem mysterious and strange.

You are probably used to the way a place, for instance the town you live in, looks completely different to you depending on your mood, your feelings. One day it is beautiful; another day it is horrible. What is inside you always changes what is outside you. In his poetry Lorca doesn't try to separate what he is feeling from what is outside him. Instead, he seems to allow what he is feeling and thinking to transform what is around him. Lorca doesn't say that the sea with moonlight on it is like a "paper sea and coin silver," but simply that a paper and coin sea exists and is there. The longed-for coast of Cuba is a "curve of sighs and clay." And he doesn't say, "I want so much to go to Cuba that it seems to me that even the trees are full of longing—the palm tree, for instance, looks as if it wants to be able to fly, to be a stork." Instead he says, "The palm tree wants to be a stork." Sometimes

Lorca just makes little lists of things, not even taking time to connect them: "Oh Cuba, oh rhythm of dried seeds! . . . Harp of living tree trunks, cayman, tobacco flower . . . Alcohol and breeze in the wheels." When Lorca wrote this way, it's unlikely that first he got the feelings and then found words to fit them. It's more likely that words and feelings occurred simultaneously. Imagine, for instance, that you're looking out the window and, without knowing why, you think about coins. If you're in one mood you might write, as Lorca does in "The Moon Rises," "silver money/sobs in the pocket." If you're in another mood, you might write, as he does in "Dawn," "Sometimes the coins in mad swarms/slam into and devour abandoned children." Both descriptions are very complicated and dramatic combinations of what is really there and what is in one's feelings. They are not realistic descriptions; they are not descriptions that you are likely to arrive at intellectually. One reason for writing in such an unrealistic and indirect way is that you can get to the strong and complex and strange kind of truth that there is, for instance, in your dreams.

Lorca thought that this kind of truth, this kind of poetry, was inspired by something he called the *duende*, a dark, overwhelming source of inspiration. The *duende* doesn't inspire gentle, intellectual poetry, but strong, dark, and passionate poetry, poetry that stays always a little mysterious and beyond you.

You may wonder, in writing so unrealistically, how you can ever tell when what you say is good or "right." The answer is that it's good when it sounds right, when it feels right, when, as you read it over, you feel convinced and excited—you may even catch your breath. This feeling of rightness will have to do with the sounds of the words, with their meanings, with their associations for you, with how they're used together. As you write poetry, you begin to understand this, but it's probably impossible to completely explain, nor do you really need to understand it in order to write in that way.

You may not at the moment or even in the next few days be filled with the *duende,* but it's interesting to try being deliberately unrealistic, as Lorca is. A good kind of poem for this is one like "Song of Black Cubans," Lorca's strange, dreamlike description of Santiago. You could choose some amazing-seeming and desirable, maybe even dangerously exciting, place to write about—and describe it in a way that may be true only for you, whatever you dream of or imagine its being like. Just start writing. If you deliberately try to fill the place with impossible things, if you make it all unreal, it will probably turn out to be real in another way, real in the way Lorca's poems are. Think of the streets and of the weather and of how the men and women are dressed. Maybe there are fountains or Ferris wheels, fireworks, strange birds. Think of the flowers and the mud and the grass and the trees, the vehicles, the lightning and thunder, the kind of music there is, the animals, the birds, and always the colors of things, the taste, the sound, the touch. A good kind of place to inspire such a poem may be a tropical city, like the Santiago Lorca writes about—a man-made and bright-colored place but with wild nature all around it, a place where you might find violent heat, palm trees filled with birds out the window, maybe even lions roaming through the hotels. You might begin by thinking of a city name that gives you the feeling of such a place—perhaps Bogotá, Acapulco, Coronado, Andalusia, Cuzco, Tongaville—or make up an exotic-sounding name. Like Lorca, you might keep saying you are going to this place and keep repeating its name—"I am going to Chichicastenango." Say in each line or in every other line what will be there, what you will see,

what you will do, how you will get there, what the ani-
mals, birds, and highways there are doing, what they
want, what is bursting forth and shining there, how the
balconies feel and the flowers in the people's hands. Use
Lorca-like lists and, if you like, his strange combinations
using *of*—"harp of living tree trunks," "curve of sighs
and clay."

W. H. Auden
(1907 – 1973)

THIS LUNAR BEAUTY

This lunar beauty
Has no history,
Is complete and early;
If beauty later
Bear any feature,
It had a lover
And is another.

This like a dream
Keeps other time,
And daytime is
The loss of this;
For time is inches
And the heart's changes,
Where ghost has haunted
Lost and wanted.

But this was never
A ghost's endeavour
Nor, finished this,
Was ghost at ease;
And till it pass

Love shall not near
The sweetness here,
Nor sorrow take
His endless look.

1 9 2 9

I

It was Easter as I walked in the public gardens,
Hearing the frogs exhaling from the pond,
Watching traffic of magnificent cloud
Moving without anxiety on open sky—
Season when lovers and writers find
An altering speech for altering things,
An emphasis on new names, on the arm
A fresh hand with fresh power.
But thinking so I came at once
Where solitary man sat weeping on a bench,
Hanging his head down, with his mouth distorted
Helpless and ugly as an embryo chicken.

So I remember all of those whose death
Is necessary condition of the season's putting forth,
Who, sorry in this time, look only back
To Christmas intimacy, a winter dialogue
Fading in silence, leaving them in tears.
And recent particulars come to mind;
The death by cancer of a once hated master,
A friend's analysis of his own failure,
Listened to at intervals throughout the winter
At different hours and in different rooms.

But always with success of others for comparison,
The happiness, for instance, of my friend Kurt Groote,
Absence of fear in Gerhart Meyer
From the sea, the truly strong man.

A 'bus ran home then, on the public ground
Lay fallen bicycles like huddled corpses:
No chattering valves of laughter emphasised
Nor the swept gown ends of a gesture stirred
The sessile hush; until a sudden shower
Fell willing into grass and closed the day,
Making choice seem a necessary error.

I I
Coming out of me living is always thinking,
Thinking changing and changing living,
Am feeling as it was seeing—
In city leaning on harbour parapet
To watch a colony of duck below
Sit, preen, and doze on buttresses
Or upright paddle on flickering stream,
Casually fishing at a passing straw.
Those find sun's luxury enough,
Shadow know not of homesick foreigner
Nor restlessness of intercepted growth.

All this time was anxiety at night,
Shooting and barricade in street.
Walking home late I listened to a friend
Talking excitedly of final war
Of proletariat against police—
That one shot girl of nineteen through the knees
They threw that one down concrete stair—
Till I was angry, said I was pleased.

Time passes in Hessen, in Gutensberg,
With hill-top and evening holds me up,
Tiny observer of enormous world.
Smoke rises from factory in field,
Memory of fire: On all sides heard
Vanishing music of isolated larks:
From village square voices in hymn,
Men's voices, an old use.
And I above standing, saying in thinking:

'Is first baby, warm in mother,
Before born and is still mother,
Time passes and now is other,
Is knowledge in him now of other,
Cries in cold air, himself no friend.
In grown man also, may see in face,
In his day-thinking and in his night-thinking,
Is wareness and is fear of other,
Alone in flesh, himself no friend.'

He says, 'We must forgive and forget,'
Forgetting saying but is unforgiving
And unforgiving is in his living;
Body reminds in him to loving,
Reminds but takes no further part,
Perfunctorily affectionate in hired room
But takes no part and is unloving
But loving death. May see in dead,
In face of dead that loving wish,
As one returns from Africa to wife
And his ancestral property in Wales.

Yet sometimes men look and say good
At strict beauty of locomotive,
Completeness of gesture or unclouded eye;
In me so absolute unity of evening

And field and distance was in me for peace
Was over me in feeling without forgetting
Those ducks' indifference, that friend's hysteria,
Without wishing and with forgiving,
To love my life, not as other,
Not as bird's life, not as child's,
'Cannot', I said, 'being no child now nor a bird.'

III

Order to stewards and the study of time,
Correct in books, was earlier than this
But joined this by the wires I watched from train,
Slackening of wire and posts' sharp reprimand,
In month of August to a cottage coming.

Being alone, the frightened soul
Returns to this life of sheep and hay
No longer his: he every hour
Moves further from this and must so move,
As child is weaned from his mother and leaves home
But taking the first steps falters, is vexed,
Happy only to find home, a place
Where no tax is levied for being there.

So, insecure, he loves and love
Is insecure, gives less than he expects.
He knows not if it be seed in time to display
Luxuriantly in a wonderful fructification
Or whether it be but a degenerate remnant
Of something immense in the past but now
Surviving only as the infectiousness of disease
Or in the malicious caricature of drunkenness;
Its end glossed over by the careless but known long
To finer perception of the mad and ill.

Moving along the track which is himself,
He loves what he hopes will last, which gone,
Begins the difficult work of mourning,
And as foreign settlers to strange country come,
By mispronunciation of native words
And intermarriage create a new race,
A new language, so may the soul
Be weaned at last to independent delight.

Startled by the violent laugh of a jay
I went from wood, from crunch underfoot,
Air between stems as under water;
As I shall leave the summer, see autumn come
Focusing stars more sharply in the sky,
See frozen buzzard flipped down the weir
And carried out to sea, leave autumn,
See winter, winter for earth and us,
A forethought of death that we may find ourselves at
        death
Not helplessly strange to the new conditions.

IV
It is time for the destruction of error.
The chairs are being brought in from the garden,
The summer talk stopped on that savage coast
Before the storms, after the guests and birds:
In sanatoriums they laugh less and less,
Less certain of cure; and the loud madman
Sinks now into a more terrible calm.

The falling children know it, the children,
At play on the fuming alkali-tip
Or by the flooded football ground know it—
This is the dragon's day, the devourer's:
Orders are given to the enemy for a time

With underground proliferation of mould,
With constant whisper and with casual question,
To haunt the poisoned in his shunned house,
To destroy the efflorescence of the flesh,
The intricate play of the mind, enforce
Conformity with the orthodox bone,
With organised fear, the articulated skeleton.

You whom I gladly walk with, touch,
Or wait for as one certain of good,
We know it, know that love
Needs more than the admiring excitement of union,
More than the abrupt self-confident farewell,
The heel on the finishing blade of grass,
The self-confidence of the falling root,
Needs death, death of the grain, our death,
Death of the old gang; would leave them
In sullen valley where is made no friend,
The old gang to be forgotten in the spring,
The hard bitch and the riding-master,
Stiff underground; deep in clear lake
The lolling bridegroom, beautiful, there.

THE WANDERER

Doom is dark and deeper than any sea-dingle.
Upon what man it fall
In spring, day-wishing flowers appearing,
Avalanche sliding, white snow from rock-face,
That he should leave his house,
No cloud-soft hand can hold him, restraint by women;

But ever that man goes
Through place-keepers, through forest trees,
A stranger to strangers over undried sea,
Houses for fishes, suffocating water,
Or lonely on fell as chat,
By pot-holed becks
A bird stone-haunting, an unquiet bird.

There head falls forward, fatigued at evening,
And dreams of home,
Waving from window, spread of welcome,
Kissing of wife under single sheet;
But waking sees
Bird-flocks nameless to him, through doorway voices
Of new men making another love.

Save him from hostile capture,
From sudden tiger's leap at corner;
Protect his house,
His anxious house where days are counted
From thunderbolt protect,
From gradual ruin spreading like a stain;
Converting number from vague to certain,
Bring joy, bring day of his returning,
Lucky with day approaching, with leaning dawn.

W. H. AUDEN

W. H. Auden had a great deal of knowledge about a great many things. He knew science, history, politics, philosophy, psychology, anthropology, art, music, literature. His poetry is full of knowledge and wisdom and ideas. Poetry, for Auden, seems a way of making real life understandable, in somewhat the way that astronomy is a way of making the real universe understandable.

The view of life in his poems is, in general, rather dark. One gets the idea that life is mostly made up of suffering, boredom, and danger; that there are momentary escapes in beauty, in friendship, in love; that there is some chance of changing it by means of prayer, devotion, and knowledge. This view permeates his poetry. He seems to write not to escape this reality, nor to idealize it, nor to find in it a mystical truth, nor to complain and place the blame, but rather to talk about it intelligently and truthfully.

However difficult life is, there is satisfaction and reassurance in understanding it. In Auden's poetry, it is as if every subject—the beauty of moonlight, the life of a friend, the feeling of love, a walk in the city, a day in the country—inspires ideas and understanding. It is as if everything he looked at and experienced brought him new wisdom. He says in "1929" that for him, "living is always thinking." And reading his poetry is a little like listening to the witty, refined, and complex conversation of a wonderfully wise teacher who, it seems, is always thinking and has thought about and decided about everything.

"This Lunar Beauty" is about a beautiful moonlit night. The moonlight inspires Auden with a rather complex idea about time and change. The time in the moonlight feels unlike other time, as the time in a dream feels unlike other time. Probably the moonlight makes time seem that way because it's a strange kind of light, light while it's dark, so it seems more like pure light. It seems complete in itself—unconnected to anything else. And that is like the beginning of time, when nothing has happened yet, when there is no history. Auden says that other beauty might seem like this lunar beauty, but it won't be, it will be like something else. It won't have this quality of suspended time. Daytime is another kind of time. Daylight, which is so different from moonlight, makes everything show. You see things in all their detail. You are aware of what used to be there that isn't there now, of how things have changed. In daylight you know that things have happened, that time is passing and has passed, that your life and your love are different from what they were. And you feel your own "history," with its ghosts. You have lost the past. You want it back. There are none of these ghosts in the moonlight. There hasn't been time for sorrow. The moonlight seems so sweet that it seems sweeter, even, than love.

"This Lunar Beauty" has very short lines, is melodious, has rather strange rhymes. The idea is expressed as a number of facts—facts told in as few words as possible, almost as in a list, without explanation, without uncertainty.

You might try writing a poem like this. It is, in general, hard to write a good poem about intellectual ideas. With ideas, you are more likely to feel an obligation to an objective "truth," and so are more likely to say what has already been said. It's hard to be as imaginative and inventive with your ideas as you are, for instance, with your feelings. W. H. Auden can help you see how to do it.

Write a poem in which something in nature inspires you with an idea. As in "This Lunar Beauty," where moonlight and daylight inspire Auden to compare two different kinds of time, two things in nature could show you two different ways of looking at something. A rose and a gardenia might give you, for instance, two different ideas about the possibility of happiness; the ocean and the sky could make you think about whether or not it is possible to change your life; the woods and a field could give you two different ideas about what success really is. This way of writing isn't as strange as it seems at first. Our abstract thoughts really are connected to the physical things around us.

It might be inspiring to write in short lines, putting a new fact, without explanation, in every line or two. Remember that in poetry you don't have to have proof that what you say is true. Just say what seems and sounds right to you. Try not to plan much in advance, maybe no more than one line at a time, and to be as free in thinking as you are in feeling. You may find, when you read the poem over, that this freedom has given it an interesting kind of logic. If you think that using rhyme would help you think of things to say, try that. In writing poetry, it is good to know how to use your intellect and your imagination at the same time.

Or write a poem like "The Wanderer." "The Wanderer" is about the dangerousness and fatedness of life in general. To talk about this, Auden uses the ancient idea of man setting forth for unknown places, and he writes about it in an old style. The dangers are made very specific—they are ancient dangers of nature, against which there is no preparation, for which there is no remedy. The poem is very formal and ceremonial, like a prayer which might be said at the man's departure and which is both a warning and a blessing. Like the hard-sounding Anglo-Saxon poetry it sounds most like, Auden's poem uses a good deal of alliteration ("Doom is dark," "head falls forward, fatigued"), omits unimportant words such as *a*, *the*, and *of*, emphasizes the obvious ("white snow," "forest trees"), and even contains a kenning, a curious kind of image which describes something in relation to its function or its purpose. The kenning here, "houses for fishes," means the ocean. One Anglo-Saxon kenning for the English Channel was "swan-raede" (swan road). The sun, turned into a kenning, might be "the man-waker." So you'd write, to say the sun shone on the English Channel, "The man-waker shone on the swan road." Try writing the poem in this kind of old style, with this kind of extreme simplicity, perhaps using Anglo-Saxon–like alliteration, leaving out all unimportant words and trying some kennings. You could make it the kind of poem that could be read at an ancient (or even a modern) ceremony—at a baptism, a marriage, on a birthday—and include both a warning and a blessing. Make the possibilities that you envision very specific—like "Avalanche sliding, white snow from rock-face," and "Bird-flocks nameless to him," and "Sudden tiger's leap at corner."

Allen Ginsberg
(1926 –   )

From Howl, *Parts I and II*

for Carl Solomon

I

I saw the best minds of my generation destroyed by
madness, starving hysterical naked,

dragging themselves through the negro streets at dawn
looking for an angry fix,

angelheaded hipsters burning for the ancient heavenly
connection to the starry dynamo in the machinery of
night

who poverty and tatters and hollow-eyed and high sat up
smoking in the supernatural darkness of cold-water
flats floating across the tops of cities contemplating
jazz,

who bared their brains to Heaven under the El and saw
Mohammedan angels staggering on tenement roofs
illuminated,

who passed through universities with radiant cool eyes
hallucinating Arkansas and Blake-light tragedy
among the scholars of war,

who were expelled from the academies for crazy & pub-
lishing obscene odes on the windows of the skull,

who cowered in unshaven rooms in underwear, burning
their money in wastebaskets and listening to the
Terror through the wall.

. . .

who chained themselves to subways for the endless ride
from Battery to holy Bronx on benzedrine until the
noise of wheels and children brought them down
shuddering mouth-wracked and battered bleak of
brain all drained of brilliance in the drear light of
Zoo,

who sank, all night in submarine light of Bickford's
floated out and sat through the stale beer afternoon
in desolate Fugazzi's, listening to the crack of doom
on the hydrogen jukebox,

who talked continuously seventy hours from park to pad
to bar to Bellvue to museum to the Brooklyn Bridge,

a lost battalion of platonic conversationalists jumping
down the stoops off fire escapes off windowsills off
Empire State out of the moon,

yacketayakking screaming vomiting whispering facts and
memories and anecdotes and eyeball kicks and
shocks of hospitals and jails and wars,

whole intellects disgorged in total recall for seven days
and nights with brilliant eyes, meat for the Syna-
gogue cast on the pavement,

who vanished into nowhere Zen New Jersey leaving a
trail of ambiguous picture postcards of Atlantic City
Hall,

suffering Eastern sweats and Tangerian bone-grindings
and migraines of China under junk-withdrawal in
Newark's bleak furnished room,

who wandered around and around at midnight in the
railroad yard wondering where to go, and went,
leaving no broken hearts,

who lit cigarettes in boxcars boxcars boxcars racketing
through snow toward lonesome farms in grandfa-
ther night,

who studied Plotinus Poe St. John of the Cross telepathy
and bop kaballa because the cosmos instinctively
vibrated at their feet in Kansas,

who loned it through the streets of Idaho seeking vision-
  ary indian angels who were visionary indian angels,

who thought they were only mad when Baltimore
  gleamed in supernatural ecstasy,

who jumped in limousines with the Chinaman of Okla-
  homa on the impulse of winter midnight streetlight
  smalltown rain,

who lounged hungry and lonesome through Houston
  seeking jazz or sex or soup, and followed the bril-
  liant Spaniard to converse about America and Eter-
  nity, a hopeless task, and so took ship to Africa,

who disappeared into the volcanoes of Mexico leaving
  behind nothing but the shadow of dungarees and
  the lava and ash of poetry scattered in fireplace Chi-
  cago,

who reappeared on the West Coast investigating the
  F.B.I. in beards and shorts with big pacifist eyes sexy
  in their dark skin passing out incomprehensible leaf-
  lets,

who burned cigarette holes in their arms protesting the
  narcotic tobacco haze of Capitalism,

who distributed Supercommunist pamphlets in Union
  Square weeping and undressing while the sirens of
  Los Alamos wailed them down, and wailed down
  Wall, and the Staten Island ferry also wailed,

who broke down crying in white gymnasiums naked and
  trembling before the machinery of other skeletons.

. . .

who faded out in vast sordid movies, were shifted in
  dreams, woke on a sudden Manhattan, and picked
  themselves up out of basements hungover with
  heartless Tokay and horrors of Third Avenue iron
  dreams & stumbled to unemployment offices,

who walked all night with their shoes full of blood on the
  snowbank docks waiting for a door in the East River
  to open to a room full of steam-heat and opium,

who created great suicidal dramas on the apartment cliff-
banks of the Hudson under the wartime blue flood-
light of the moon & their heads shall be crowned
with laurel in oblivion,

who ate the lamb stew of the imagination or digested the
crab at the muddy bottom of the rivers of Bowery,

who wept at the romance of the streets with their push-
carts full of onions and bad music,

who sat in boxes breathing in the darkness under the
bridge, and rose up to build harpsichords in their
lofts,

who coughed on the sixth floor of Harlem crowned with
flame under the tubercular sky surrounded by or-
ange crates of theology,

who scribbled all night rocking and rolling over lofty
incantations which in the yellow morning were stan-
zas of gibberish,

who cooked rotten animals lung heart feet tail borsht
& tortillas dreaming of the pure vegetable king-
dom,

who plunged themselves under meat trucks looking for
an egg,

who threw their watches off the roof to cast their ballot
for Eternity outside of Time, & alarm clocks fell on
their heads every day for the next decade,

who cut their wrists three times successively unsuccess-
fully, gave up and were forced to open antique
stores where they thought they were growing old
and cried,

who were burned alive in their innocent flannel suits on
Madison Avenue amid blasts of leaden verse & the
tanked-up clatter of the iron regiments of fashion &
the nitroglycerine shrieks of the fairies of advertis-
ing & the mustard gas of sinister intelligent editors,
or were run down by the drunken taxicabs of Abso-
lute Reality,

who jumped off the Brooklyn Bridge this actually hap-
   pened and walked away unknown and forgotten into
   the ghostly daze of Chinatown soup alleyways &
   firetrucks, not even one free beer,

who sang out of their windows in despair, fell out of the
   subway window, jumped in the filthy Passaic, leaped
   on negroes, cried all over the street, danced on bro-
   ken wineglasses barefoot smashed phonograph rec-
   ords of nostalgic European 1930's German jazz
   finished the whiskey and threw up groaning into the
   bloody toilet, moans in their ears and the blast of
   colossal steamwhistles,

who barreled down the highways of the past journeying
   to each other's hotrod-Golgotha jail-solitude watch
   or Birmingham jazz incarnation,

who drove crosscountry seventytwo hours to find out if
   I had a vision or you had a vision or he had a vision
   to find out Eternity,

who journeyed to Denver, who died in Denver, who
   came back to Denver & waited in vain, who watched
   over Denver & brooded & loned in Denver and
   finally went away to find out the Time, & now Den-
   ver is lonesome for her heroes,

who fell on their knees in hopeless cathedrals praying for
   each other's salvation and light and breasts, until the
   soul illuminated its hair for a second,

who crashed through their minds in jail waiting for im-
   possible criminals with golden heads and the charm
   of reality in their hearts who sang sweet blues to
   Alcatraz,

who retired to Mexico to cultivate a habit, or Rocky
   Mount to tender Buddha or Tangiers to boys or
   Southern Pacific to the black locomotive or Harvard
   to Narcissus to Woodlawn to the daisychain or
   grave,

who demanded sanity trials accusing the radio of hypno-
tism & were left with their insanity & their hands &
a hung jury,

who threw potato salad at CCNY lecturers on Dadaism
and subsequently presented themselves on the
granite steps of the madhouse with shaven heads
and harlequin speech of suicide, demanding instan-
taneous lobotomy,

and who were given instead the concrete void of insulin
metrasol electricity hydrotherapy psychotherapy oc-
cupational therapy pingpong & amnesia,

who in humorless protest overturned only one symbolic
pingpong table, resting briefly in catatonia,

returning years later truly bald except for a wig of blood,
and tears and fingers, to the visible madman doom
of the wards of the madtowns of the East,

Pilgrim State's Rockland's and Greystone's foetid halls,
bickering with the echoes of the soul, rocking and
rolling in the midnight solitude-bench dolmen-
realms of love, dream of life a nightmare, bodies
turned to stone as heavy as the moon,

with mother finally ******, and the last fantastic book
flung out of the tenement window, and the last door
closed at 4 AM and the last telephone slammed at the
wall in reply and the last furnished room emptied
down to the last piece of mental furniture, a yellow
paper rose twisted on a wire hanger in the closet,
and even that imaginary, nothing but a hopeful little
bit of hallucination—

ah, Carl, while you are not safe I am not safe, and now
you're really in the total animal soup of time—

and who therefore ran through the icy streets obsessed
with a sudden flash of the alchemy of the use
of the ellipse the catalog the meter & the vibrating
plane,

who dreamt and made incarnate gaps in Time & Space
through images juxtaposed, and trapped the arch-
angel of the soul between 2 visual images and joined
the elemental verbs and set the noun and dash of
consciousness together jumping with sensation of
Pater Omnipotens Aeterna Deus

to recreate the syntax and measure of poor human prose
and stand before you speechless and intelligent and
shaking with shame, rejected yet confessing out the
soul to conform to the rhythm of thought in his
naked and endless head,

the madman bum and angel beat in Time, unknown, yet
putting down here what might be left to say in time
come after death,

and rose reincarnate in the ghostly clothes of jazz in the
goldhorn shadow of the band and blew the suffering
of America's naked mind for love into an eli eli
lamma lamma sabacthani saxophone cry that shiv-
ered the cities down to the last radio

with the absolute heart of the poem of life butchered out
of their own bodies good to eat a thousand years.

II

What sphinx of cement and aluminum bashed open their
skulls and ate up their brains and imagination?

Moloch! Solitude! Filth! Ugliness! Ashcans and unob-
tainable dollars! Children screaming under the
stairways! Boys sobbing in armies! Old men weep-
ing in the parks!

Moloch! Moloch! Nightmare of Moloch! Moloch the
loveless! Mental Moloch! Moloch the heavy judger
of men!

Moloch the incomprehensible prison! Moloch the cross-
bone soulless jailhouse and Congress of sorrows!
Moloch whose buildings are judgment! Moloch the
vast stone of war! Moloch the stunned govern-
ments!

Moloch whose mind is pure machinery! Moloch whose blood is running money! Moloch whose fingers are ten armies! Moloch whose breast is a cannibal dynamo! Moloch whose ear is a smoking tomb!

Moloch whose eyes are a thousand blind windows! Moloch whose skyscrapers stand in the long streets like endless Jehovahs! Moloch whose factories dream and croak in the fog! Moloch whose smokestacks and antennae crown the cities!

Moloch whose love is endless oil and stone! Moloch whose soul is electricity and banks! Moloch whose poverty is the specter of genius! Moloch whose fate is a cloud of sexless hydrogen! Moloch whose name is the Mind!

. . .

They broke their backs lifting Moloch to Heaven! Pavements, trees, radios, tons! lifting the city to Heaven which exists and is everywhere about us!

Visions! omens! hallucinations! miracles! ecstasies! gone down the American river!

Dreams! adorations! illuminations! religions! the whole boatload of sensitive bullshit!

Breakthroughs! over the river! flips and crucifixions! gone down the flood! Highs! Epiphanies! Despairs! Ten years' animal screams and suicides! Minds! New loves! Mad generation! down on the rocks of Time!

Real holy laughter in the river! They saw it all! the wild eyes! the holy yells! They bade farewell! They jumped off the roof! to solitude! waving! carrying flowers! Down to the river! into the street!

. . .

A SUPERMARKET IN CALIFORNIA

What thoughts I have of you tonight, Walt Whitman, for I walked down the sidestreets under the trees with a headache self-conscious looking at the full moon.

In my hungry fatigue, and shopping for images, I went into the neon fruit supermarket, dreaming of your enumerations!

What peaches and what penumbras! Whole families shopping at night! Aisles full of husbands! Wives in the avocados, babies in the tomatoes!—and you, García Lorca, what were you doing down by the watermelons?

I saw you, Walt Whitman, childless, lonely old grubber, poking among the meats in the refrigerator and eyeing the grocery boys.

I heard you asking questions of each: Who killed the pork chops? What price bananas? Are you my Angel?

I wandered in and out of the brilliant stacks of cans following you, and followed in my imagination by the store detective.

We strode down the open corridors together in our solitary fancy tasting artichokes, possessing every frozen delicacy, and never passing the cashier.

Where are we going, Walt Whitman? The doors close in an hour. Which way does your beard point tonight?

(I touch your book and dream of our odyssey in the supermarket and feel absurd.)

Will we walk all night through solitary streets? The trees add shade to shade, lights out in the houses, we'll both be lonely.

Will we stroll dreaming of the lost America of love past blue automobiles in driveways, home to our silent cottage?

Ah, dear father, graybeard, lonely old courage-teacher, what America did you have when Charon quit poling his ferry and you got out on a smoking bank and stood watching the boat disappear on the black waters of Lethe?

ALLEN GINSBERG

Allen Ginsberg's poetry has two main subjects: the excitement, variety, violence, and turbulence of the physical, intellectual, and emotional life he sees around him, and the beautiful, secret, mystical vision of peace and truth that he is always looking for, both beyond this violent life and within it. His poems are often about the search for, or the finding of, the mystical truth. But the search is often a terrible, violent, crazy (if exhilarating) search.

Like T. S. Eliot, Ginsberg is a poet who responds directly to the social and political world in his poetry, but his response to it is much more personal and autobiographical; he responds not as a created character, like Prufrock, but as Allen Ginsberg, the real, living, particular, inspired one who was born in New Jersey and went to Columbia University. He tells us a lot about himself —nothing seems too personal to put in a poem.

When Allen Ginsberg published his first long poem, *Howl*, in 1956, it interested and excited many people. He had written a poem of an entirely new kind about an entirely new subject matter: the sick, painful, frustrated, dangerous lives of his friends, people who were brilliant and artistic but who felt crushed and desperate, even to the point of being suicidal. They wanted to find beauty and meaning, and couldn't find it in the ordinary, normal kind of American life they saw around them. So they looked for it elsewhere, desperately, in drugs, in alcohol, in sex, going from one city to another, always looking for the secret, the mystical experience, and almost always ending up impoverished, hurt, sick, down and out, sometimes insane, sometimes dead. The first part of *Howl* presents, in almost every one of its very long lines, different pictures of these people, different scenes in their search. *Howl* shows them as heroes, with their search for a new truth meaning (as such a search usually does) a battle against the old one.

Though *Howl* is about people who are hurt and ruined, "destroyed by madness, starving hysterical naked," it doesn't sound sorrowful, solemn, and sad, but exultant, exuberant, and energetic. Ginsberg writes about his friends with tremendous energy, excitement, and even humor. The lines are crowded with words, crowded with hundreds of variations on what these people are like and what they do. The poem is as much about their brilliance and their excitement and their mystical fervor and their wild, beautiful hope for the truth as it is about the terrible things that happen to them. Ginsberg puts words together in a way that makes the dangerous and difficult physical world of these people and their beautiful visions present at the same time: "angel-headed hipsters," "supernatural darkness of cold-water flats," "Zen New Jersey," "Baltimore gleam(ing) in supernatural ecstasy," "orange crates of theology." It is as if their lives are some precious kind of energy that can change the world. And the poem is like an account of some crazy, unstoppable pilgrimage. It is written almost like a litany or a chant.

The lives of most people aren't as desperate and intensely single-minded, whatever their convictions, as those of the group which Allen Ginsberg pictures in *Howl*. Most people, though, informally or otherwise, are part of some group or other which shares certain interests, dreams, ideas, struggles. Maybe what they have in common is intellectual, maybe it is artistic, maybe social, maybe revolutionary in one way or another. Such groups do certain things that separate them from other people —they wear a certain kind of clothes, go to certain places and not others, talk a certain way.

Write a poem in something of the style of *Howl,*

about a group of your friends (yourself included if you wish) or any other group of people you know, or about a group of people that you don't know but imagine. Try writing in very long lines. Make each line a certain scene in these people's lives—a scene typical more of the way they all act than of how just one of them acts—on the street, in a bar, in a living room, on a bridge, in a vacant lot, in a car, in a drugstore, at the movies, at a party, in a classroom. It may help give it a powerful, litany-like style if you exaggerate everything these people do together and completely leave out the lives they live separately. Give names of streets, towns, hangouts, everything, crowding into every line many details of the scene. However inconsequential the things they do may seem at certain times, you might try making the poem heroic, acting as if everything they do were part of some pilgrimage, some mission. Don't worry about punctuation or connections or making perfect sense; more important is the excitement, the putting together of great lists of vivid, harsh, particular details—as in Ginsberg's description of his friends, who "chained themselves to subways for the endless ride from Battery to holy Bronx on benzedrine until the noise of wheels and children brought them down shuddering mouth-wracked and battered bleak of brain all drained of brilliance in the drear light of Zoo." Make their thoughts, their beliefs, their talk, all part of the scene you describe. You might want to start every line, or almost every line, with the same word or words, as Ginsberg starts many of his with *who*.

Frank O'Hara

(1926–1966)

A TRUE ACCOUNT OF
TALKING TO THE SUN
AT FIRE ISLAND

The Sun woke me this morning loud
and clear, saying "Hey! I've been
trying to wake you up for fifteen
minutes. Don't be so rude, you are
only the second poet I've ever chosen
to speak to personally

                 so why
aren't you more attentive? If I could
burn you through the window I would
to wake you up. I can't hang around
here all day."

              "Sorry, Sun, I stayed
up late last night talking to Hal."

"When I woke up Mayakovsky he was
a lot more prompt" the Sun said
petulantly. "Most people are up
already waiting to see if I'm going
to put in an appearance."

                              I tried
to apologize "I missed you yesterday."
"That's better" he said. "I didn't
know you'd come out." "You may be
wondering why I've come so close?"
"Yes" I said beginning to feel hot
wondering if maybe he wasn't burning me
anyway.
              "Frankly I wanted to tell you
I like your poetry. I see a lot
on my rounds and you're okay. You may
not be the greatest thing on earth, but
you're different. Now, I've heard some
say you're crazy, they being excessively
calm themselves to my mind, and other
crazy poets think that you're a boring
reactionary. Not me.
                          Just keep on
like I do and pay no attention. You'll
find that people always will complain
about the atmosphere, either too hot
or too cold too bright or too dark, days
too short or too long.
                          If you don't appear
at all one day they think you're lazy
or dead. Just keep right on, I like it.
And don't worry about your lineage
poetic or natural. The Sun shines on
the jungle, you know, on the tundra
the sea, the ghetto. Wherever you were
I knew it and saw you moving. I was waiting
for you to get to work.

                          And now that you
are making your own days, so to speak,
even if no one reads you but me

you won't be depressed. Not
everyone can look up, even at me. It
hurts their eyes."
        "Oh Sun, I'm so grateful to you!"

"Thanks and remember I'm watching. It's
easier for me to speak to you out
here. I don't have to slide down
between buildings to get your ear.
I know you love Manhattan, but
you ought to look up more often.
            And
always embrace things, people earth
sky stars, as I do, freely and with
the appropriate sense of space. That
is your inclination, known in the heavens
and you should follow it to hell, if
necessary, which I doubt.
         Maybe we'll
speak again in Africa, of which I too
am specially fond. Go back to sleep now
Frank, and I may leave a tiny poem
in that brain of yours as my farewell."

"Sun, don't go!" I was awake
at last. "No, go I must, they're calling
me."
      "Who are they?"
           Rising he said "Some
day you'll know. They're calling to you
too." Darkly he rose, and then I slept.

THE DAY LADY DIED

It is 12:20 in New York a Friday
three days after Bastille day, yes
it is 1959 and I go get a shoeshine
because I will get off the 4:19 in Easthampton
at 7:15 and then go straight to dinner
and I don't know the people who will feed me

I walk up the muggy street beginning to sun
and have a hamburger and a malted and buy
an ugly NEW WORLD WRITING to see what the poets
in Ghana are doing these days
                        I go on to the bank
and Miss Stillwagon (first name Linda I once heard)
doesn't even look up my balance for once in her life
and in the GOLDEN GRIFFIN I get a little Verlaine
for Patsy with drawings by Bonnard although I do
think of Hesiod, trans. Richmond Lattimore or
Brendan Behan's new play or *Le Balcon* or *Les Nègres*
of Genet, but I don't, I stick with Verlaine
after practically going to sleep with quandariness

and for Mike I just stroll into the PARK LANE
Liquor Store and ask for a bottle of Strega and
then I go back where I came from to 6th Avenue
and the tobacconist in the Ziegfeld Theatre and
casually ask for a carton of Gauloises and a carton
of Picayunes, and a NEW YORK POST with her face on it

and I am sweating a lot by now and thinking of
leaning on the john door in the 5 SPOT
while she whispered a song along the keyboard
to Mal Waldron and everyone and I stopped breathing

A TERRESTRIAL CUCKOO

What a hot day it is! for
Jane and me above the scorch
of sun on jungle waters to be
paddling up and down the Essequibo
in our canoe of war-surplus gondola parts.

We enjoy it, though: the bats squeak
in our wrestling hair, parakeets
bungle lightly into gorges of blossom,
the water's full of gunk and
what you might call waterlilies if you're

silly as we. Our intuitive craft
our striped T shirts and shorts
cry out to vines that are feasting
on flies to make straight the way
of tropical art. "I'd give a lempira or two

to have it all slapped onto a
canvas" says Jane. "How like
lazy flamingos look the floating
weeds! and the infundibuliform
corolla on our right's a harmless Charybdis!

or am I seduced by its ambient
mauve?" The nose of our vessel sneezes
into a bundle of amaryllis, quite
artificially tied with ribbon.
Are there people nearby? and postcards?

We, essentially travelers, frown
and backwater. What will the savages
think if our friends turn up? with

sunglasses and cuneiform decoders!
probably. Oh Jane, is there no more frontier?

We strip off our pretty blazers
of tapa and dive like salamanders
into the vernal stream. Alas! they
have left the jungle aflame, and in
friendly chatter of Kotzebue and Salonika our

friends swiftly retreat downstream
on a flowery float. We strike through
the tongues and tigers hotly, towards
orange mountains, black taboos, dada!
and clouds. To return with absolute treasure!

our only penchant, that. And a red-
billed toucan, pointing t'aurora highlands
and caravanserais of junk, cries out
"New York is everywhere like Paris!
go back when you're rich, behung with lice!"

TO THE FILM INDUSTRY IN CRISIS

Not you, lean quarterlies and swarthy periodicals
with your studious incursions toward the pomposity of
    ants,
nor you, experimental theatre in which Emotive Fruition
is wedding Poetic Insight perpetually, nor you,
promenading Grand Opera, obvious as an ear (though
    you
are close to my heart), but you, Motion Picture Industry,
it's you I love!

In times of crisis, we must all decide again and again
   whom we love.
And give credit where it's due: not to my starched nurse,
   who taught me
how to be bad and not bad rather than good (and has
   lately availed
herself of this information), not to the Catholic Church
which is at best an oversolemn introduction to cosmic
   entertainment,
not to the American Legion, which hates everybody, but
   to you,
glorious Silver Screen, tragic Technicolor, amorous
   Cinemascope,
stretching Vistavision and startling Stereophonic Sound,
   with all
your heavenly dimensions and reverberations and icono-
   clasms! To
Richard Barthelmess as the "tol'able" boy barefoot and
   in pants,
Jeanette MacDonald of the flaming hair and lips and
   long, long neck,
Sue Carroll as she sits for eternity on the damaged
   fender of a car
and smiles, Ginger Rogers with her pageboy bob like a
   sausage
on her shuffling shoulders, peach-melba–voiced Fred
   Astaire of the feet,
Eric von Stroheim, the seducer of mountain-climbers'
   gasping spouses,
the Tarzans, each and every one of you (I cannot bring
   myself to prefer
Johnny Weissmuller to Lex Barker, I cannot!), Mae West
   in a furry sled,
her bordello radiance and bland remarks, Rudolph
   Valentino of the moon,
its crushing passions, and moonlike, too, the gentle
   Norma Shearer,

Miriam Hopkins dropping her champagne glass off Joel
    McCrea's yacht
and crying into the dappled sea, Clark Gable rescuing
    Gene Tierney
from Russia and Allan Jones rescuing Kitty Carlisle from
    Harpo Marx,
Cornel Wilde coughing blood on the piano keys while
    Merle Oberon berates,
Marilyn Monroe in her little spike heels reeling through
    Niagara Falls,
Joseph Cotten puzzling and Orson Welles puzzled and
    Dolores del Rio
eating orchids for lunch and breaking mirrors, Gloria
    Swanson reclining,
and Jean Harlow reclining and wiggling, and Alice Faye
    reclining
and wiggling and singing, Myrna Loy being calm and
    wise, William Powell
in his stunning urbanity, Elizabeth Taylor blossoming,
    yes, to you

and to all you others, the great, the near-great, the fea-
    tured, the extras
who pass quickly and return in dreams saying your one
    or two lines,
my love!
Long may you illumine space with your marvellous ap-
    pearances, delays
and enunciations, and may the money of the world glit-
    teringly cover you
as you rest after a long day under the kleig lights with
    your faces
in packs for our edification, the way the clouds come
    often at night
but the heavens operate on the star system. It is a divine
    precedent
you perpetuate! Roll on, reels of celluloid, as the great
    earth rolls on!

POEM

Hate is only one of many responses
true, hurt and hate go hand in hand
but why be afraid of hate, it is only there

think of filth, is it really awesome
neither is hate
don't be shy of unkindness, either
it's cleansing and allows you to be direct
like an arrow that feels something

out and out meanness, too, lets love breathe
you don't have to fight off getting in too deep
you can always get out if you're not too scared

an ounce of prevention's
enough to poison the heart
don't think of others
until you have thought of yourself, are true
all of these things, if you feel them
will be graced by a certain reluctance
and turn into gold

if felt by me, will be smilingly deflected
by your mysterious concern

SLEEPING ON THE WING

Perhaps it is to avoid some great sadness,
as in a Restoration tragedy the hero cries "Sleep!
O for a long sound sleep and so forget it!"
that one flies, soaring above the shoreless city,
veering upward from the pavement as a pigeon
does when a car honks or a door slams, the door
of dreams, life perpetuated in parti-colored loves
and beautiful lies all in different languages.
Fear drops away too, like the cement, and you
are over the Atlantic. Where is Spain? where is
who? The Civil War was fought to free the slaves,
was it? A sudden down-draught reminds you of gravity
and your position in respect to human love. But
here is where the gods are, speculating, bemused.
Once you are helpless, you are free, can you believe
that? Never to waken to the sad struggle of a face?
to travel always over some impersonal vastness,
to be out of, forever, neither in nor for!

The eyes roll asleep as if turned by the wind
and the lids flutter open slightly like a wing.
The world is an iceberg, so much is invisible!
and was and is, and yet the form, it may be sleeping
too. Those features etched in the ice of someone
loved who died, you are a sculptor dreaming of space
and speed, your hand alone could have done this.
Curiosity, the passionate hand of desire. Dead,
or sleeping? Is there speed enough? And, swooping,
you relinquish all that you have made your own,
the kingdom of your self sailing, for you must awake
and breathe your warmth in this beloved image
whether it's dead or merely disappearing,
as space is disappearing and your singularity.

FRANK O'HARA

Small personal details—such as the time you wake up, the books you buy, who calls on the phone, what clothes you wear—actually make up a rather large part of experience, and matter a lot, but they aren't usually put into poetry—they don't seem important enough or general enough. How can these things matter to anyone except the person who experiences them? Frank O'Hara puts them into his poetry for their own sake; they are simply there, as important as anything else. They are obviously related to larger ideas and feelings (what isn't?), but the connection isn't insisted on. You get the feeling, reading Frank O'Hara, that anything and everything you think or see or feel can be put in a poem and it will work out right. He seems to write from the middle of all these things, before they have been divided into subjects and ideas, while they are still part of ordinary unsorted-out days. Sometimes his poems seem, in fact, to be more about particular days than about particular subjects.

Instead of beginning with a subject, it often seems as though Frank O'Hara began a poem just by starting to write as a person begins a conversation just by starting to talk. Subjects, ideas, and perceptions come up in his poems the way they do in thinking and in conversation, one after another, both connected and unconnected to everything else that is going on. When particular people or towns or streets or books appear in his poems, he lets them stay particular, the way they really are, with their real names—Patsy and Easthampton and Sixth Avenue and *New World Writing.* And he leaves himself in the middle of it all, walking, thinking, looking around, and talking. His poems don't give profound explanations for the way life is—they give a feeling of what it's like to be alive.

"Sleeping on the Wing" is a poem with a dream in it. The dream seems to have taken place during one of those sleeps, maybe in the afternoon, in which you don't quite lose completely your awareness of your real life, when you stay a little in between your dreams and your real concerns. The dream in the poem is about flying. The concerns seem to be mainly about the death of someone the poet loved.

The poem is a little hard to read until you get used to the way O'Hara lets the details of his thoughts flow into one another, the way they probably really did during his sleep. He goes to sleep suddenly, as suddenly as a pigeon flies up when a car honks or when a door slams. For him, the door that has slammed is "the door/of dreams," and he is the one flying up, over the city, out toward the Atlantic. Like the hero of a tragedy for whom everything has gotten to be too much, he sleeps to forget. Sleeping is a way to get away, as in his dreams flying is a way to get away—from the city, from the cement, from fear, from facts (about Spain, about the Civil War, about anything). It is a way to be in a "beautiful lie"— to be as calmly distant as the Greek gods were on Mount Olympus, to be really free, over the "impersonal vastness" of the sea. In a way it would seem good to stay "away" forever, away from caring about people, and feeling confused, and being hurt.

But even in his dream a "down-draught" reminds him that just as gravity is a force that holds you to the earth, so is love. Both keep you from flying, from being free. In his dream he flies so far away that the world seems an iceberg below him. Or perhaps its "form"—the way it really is—is asleep, the way he is, as you could think the form of a statue was still "sleeping" (still uncarved) inside a block of marble. Now the face of the person who died is carved in the ice. Frank O'Hara says he himself is the sculptor, that is, he is the one who made these features appear. And in fact he did, since they are appearing in his dream—brought to his mind by feelings of wonder and curiosity and desire. But who really is dead and who is sleeping? Can he fly with enough speed to wake up? And he swoops back down, to earth, to being awake, to being alive, to remembering the loved person's reality and life and death. His flight, in which he was so distant and exceptional and free, disappears, as does the space he flew through and the image he carved.

"Sleeping on the Wing" says a great deal in a short space. It says, for one thing, a lot about the amazing confusion of desires that people have at various times. Do we want to be asleep or awake, to forget or remember, to be alone or with people, attached or free, away or in the middle of things, to be indifferent or to love and thus risk pain? The poem doesn't try to explain it all; rather, it gives a sense of what it's like to be in the middle of an inexplicable combination of feelings. If Frank O'Hara had tried to sort it all out in advance, he probably couldn't have gotten to this same sense. Our intellect is relatively slow in getting to the truth of feelings. Our dreams every night illustrate how fast and accurate we can be with another part of our minds.

Frank O'Hara said in an essay about writing, "You just go on your nerve." And to get to the brilliant, concise, honest kind of sense there is in "Sleeping on the Wing," you probably have to give up advance planning and logic and restraint, and trust your nerve.

Write a poem that has a dream in it. Start from anywhere—from a detail in the dream, or just from a thought. The important thing isn't to get the plot of the dream just right. The idea is to use the dream (some of it or all of it) to write a poem. Be as casual about the details of the dream as you are about your other thoughts. As you write, let the poem be open to thoughts, associations, whatever comes to mind, even if they seem, at the moment, trivial, strange, silly, incomplete, or disconnected. Whenever anything in the dream makes you think of something—an idea, a feeling, a memory—say it. Like O'Hara's poem, yours can be a combination of dreams and of thinking. One thing that might help you to get in a mood of dreamy concentration is to write while listening to music (Frank O'Hara often did this). Remember, nothing that you write has to be final—you can always change the poem later.

Another kind of poem to write is a poem in which the subject is a day, like Frank O'Hara's "The Day Lady Died." O'Hara's poem is about a day of doing a lot of ordinary things, then finding out something extraordinary: that someone who meant a lot to him has died. The ordinary things he does are in preparation for going to the country for the weekend to stay with friends (Mike and Patsy): he gets money from the bank, buys presents for his hosts. Then he does another ordinary thing—buys a newspaper—and finds out something very bad and not ordinary—that the singer Billie Holiday has just died. "Lady Day," which the title of the poem refers to, was a name Billie Holiday was called by her admirers. He feels shocked and unhappy and is overcome by the memory of the last time he saw her, when she was singing at a night club called The Five Spot.

Your poem about a day might be about a completely ordinary day or, like O'Hara's, an ordinary day on which one extraordinary thing happened—something that happened to you, something you thought, something you found out. If you do end with something like that, be sure to make it just one in a list with the others, described plainly and not prepared for with any special buildup. It will probably be clear which things are more and less important to you; and, also, you can refer to it in your title, as Frank O'Hara does. In any case, just start talking about this ordinary or mostly ordinary day without deciding in advance what is going to come next. Let the poem surprise you a little, like a walk you take when you're going nowhere in particular. Let the poem start sometime at the beginning of the day. Try making it a rule that you'll put a name of someone or something in every line—use the names of streets, bridges, friends, movie stars, restaurants, soft drinks, rivers, magazines, whatever. That is, instead of saying "We walk down the street," say "Jennie and I walk down Cypress Road." You can write it in the present as if you were still in the middle of it, saying what you do, what you're thinking, what you remember, what the weather is like, what you're wearing, what you say, what you see. If you revise the poem, one way to decide what you really want to be in it is to decide what seems to be part of the real feeling and mood of that day.

John Ashbery
(1927 – 　　)

THE INSTRUCTION MANUAL

As I sit looking out of a window of the building
I wish I did not have to write the instruction manual on
    the uses of a new metal.
I look down into the street and see people, each walking
    with an inner peace,
And envy them—they are so far away from me!
Not one of them has to worry about getting out this
    manual on schedule.
And, as my way is, I begin to dream, resting my elbows
    on the desk and leaning out of the window a little,
Of dim Guadalajara! City of rose-colored flowers!
City I wanted most to see, and most did not see, in
    Mexico!
But I fancy I see, under the press of having to write the
    instruction manual,
Your public square, city, with its elaborate little band-
    stand!
The band is playing *Scheherazade* by Rimsky-Korsakov.
Around stand the flower girls, handing out rose- and
    lemon-colored flowers,
Each attractive in her rose-and-blue striped dress (Oh!
    such shades of rose and blue),

And nearby is the little white booth where women in
   green serve you green and yellow fruit.
The couples are parading; everyone is in a holiday mood.
First, leading the parade, is a dapper fellow
Clothed in deep blue. On his head sits a white hat
And he wears a mustache, which has been trimmed for
   the occasion.
His dear one, his wife, is young and pretty; her shawl is
   rose, pink, and white.
Her slippers are patent leather, in the American fashion,
And she carries a fan, for she is modest, and does not
   want the crowd to see her face too often.
But everybody is so busy with his wife or loved one
I doubt they would notice the mustachioed man's wife.
Here come the boys! They are skipping and throwing
   little things on the sidewalk
Which is made of gray tile. One of them, a little older,
   has a toothpick in his teeth.
He is silenter than the rest, and affects not to notice the
   pretty young girls in white.
But his friends notice them, and shout their jeers at the
   laughing girls.
Yet soon all this will cease, with the deepening of their
   years,
And love bring each to the parade grounds for another
   reason.
But I have lost sight of the young fellow with the tooth-
   pick.
Wait—there he is—on the other side of the bandstand,
Secluded from his friends, in earnest talk with a young
   girl
Of fourteen or fifteen. I try to hear what they are saying
But it seems they are just mumbling something—shy
   words of love, probably.
She is slightly taller than he, and looks quietly down into
   his sincere eyes.

She is wearing white. The breeze ruffles her long fine
    black hair against her olive cheek.
Obviously she is in love. The boy, the young boy with the
    toothpick, he is in love too;
His eyes show it. Turning from this couple,
I see there is an intermission in the concert.
The paraders are resting and sipping drinks through
    straws
(The drinks are dispensed from a large glass crock by a
    lady in dark blue),
And the musicians mingle among them, in their creamy
    white uniforms, and talk
About the weather, perhaps, or how their kids are doing
    at school.

Let us take this opportunity to tiptoe into one of the side
    streets.
Here you may see one of those white houses with green
    trim
That are so popular here. Look—I told you!
It is cool and dim inside, but the patio is sunny.
An old woman in gray sits there, fanning herself with a
    palm leaf fan.
She welcomes us to her patio, and offers us a cooling
    drink.
"My son is in Mexico City," she says. "He would wel-
    come you too
If he were here. But his job is with a bank there.
Look, here is a photograph of him."
And a dark-skinned lad with pearly teeth grins out at us
    from the worn leather frame.
We thank her for her hospitality, for it is getting late
And we must catch a view of the city, before we leave,
    from a good high place.
That church tower will do—the faded pink one, there
    against the fierce blue of the sky. Slowly we enter.

The caretaker, an old man dressed in brown and gray,
asks us how long we have been in the city, and how
we like it here.
His daughter is scrubbing the steps—she nods to us as
we pass into the tower.
Soon we have reached the top, and the whole network of
the city extends before us.
There is the rich quarter, with its houses of pink and
white, and its crumbling, leafy terraces.
There is the poorer quarter, its homes a deep blue.
There is the market, where men are selling hats and
swatting flies.
And there is the public library, painted several shades of
pale green and beige.
Look! There is the square we just came from, with the
promenaders.
There are fewer of them, now that the heat of the day has
increased,
But the young boy and girl still lurk in the shadows of the
bandstand.
And there is the home of the little old lady—
She is still sitting in the patio, fanning herself.
How limited, but how complete withal, has been our
experience of Guadalajara!
We have seen young love, married love, and the love of
an aged mother for her son.
We have heard the music, tasted the drinks, and looked
at colored houses.
What more is there to do, except stay? And that we
cannot do.
And as a last breeze freshens the top of the weathered
old tower, I turn my gaze
Back to the instruction manual which has made me
dream of Guadalajara.

HE

He cuts down the lakes so they appear straight
He smiles at his feet in their tired mules.
He turns up the music much louder.
He takes down the vaseline from the pantry shelf.

He is the capricious smile behind the colored bottles.
He eats not lest the poor want some.
He breathes of attitudes the piney altitudes.
He indeed is the White Cliffs of Dover.

He knows that his neck is frozen.
He snorts in the vale of dim wolves.
He writes to say, "If ever you visit this island,
He'll grow you back to your childhood.

"He is the liar behind the hedge
He grew one morning out of candor.
He is his own consolation prize.
He has had his eye on you from the beginning."

He hears the weak cut down with a smile.
He waltzes tragically on the spitting housetops.
He is never near. What you need
He cancels with the air of one making a salad.

He is always the last to know.
He is strength you once said was your bonnet.
He has appeared in "Carmen."
He is after us. If you decide

He is important, it will get you nowhere.
He is the source of much bitter reflection.

He used to be pretty for a rat.
He is now over-proud of his Etruscan appearance.

He walks in his sleep into your life.
He is worth knowing only for the children
He has reared as savages in Utah.
He helps his mother take in the clothes-line.

He is unforgettable as a shooting star.
He is known as "Liverlips."
He will tell you he has had a bad time of it.
He will try to pretend his press agent is a temptress.

He looks terrible on the stairs.
He cuts himself on what he eats.
He was last seen flying to New York.
He was handing out cards which read:

"He wears a question in his left eye.
He dislikes the police but will associate with them.
He will demand something not on the menu.
He is invisible to the eyes of beauty and culture.

"He prevented the murder of Mistinguett in Mexico.
He has a knack for abortions. If you see
He is following you, forget him immediately:
He is dangerous even though asleep and unarmed."

OUR YOUTH

Of bricks . . . Who built it? Like some crazy balloon
When love leans on us

Its nights . . . The velvety pavement sticks to our feet.
The dead puppies turn us back on love.

Where we are. Sometimes
The brick arches led to a room like a bubble, that broke
    when you entered it
And sometimes to a fallen leaf.
We got crazy with emotion, showing how much we knew.

The Arabs took us. We knew
The dead horses. We were discovering coffee,
How it is to be drunk hot, with bare feet
In Canada. And the immortal music of Chopin

Which we had been discovering for several months
Since we were fourteen years old. And coffee grounds,
And the wonder of hands, and the wonder of the day
When the child discovers her first dead hand.

Do you know it? Hasn't she
Observed you too? Haven't you been observed to her?
My, haven't the flowers been? Is the evil
In't? What window? What did you say there?

Heh? Eh? Our youth is dead.
From the minute we discover it with eyes closed
Advancing into mountain light.
Ouch . . . You will never have that young boy,

That boy with the monocle
Could have been your father
He is passing by. No, that other one,
Upstairs. He is the one who wanted to see you.

He is dead. Green and yellow handkerchiefs cover him.
Perhaps he will never rot, I see

That my clothes are dry. I will go.
The naked girl crosses the street.

Blue hampers . . . Explosions,
Ice . . . The ridiculous
Vases of porphyry. All that our youth
Can't use, that it was created for.

It's true we have not avoided our destiny
By weeding out the old people.
Our faces have filled with smoke. We escape
Down the cloud ladder, but the problem has not been
    solved.

THE PAINTER

Sitting between the sea and the buildings
He enjoyed painting the sea's portrait.
But just as children imagine a prayer
Is merely silence, he expected his subject
To rush up the sand, and, seizing a brush,
Plaster its own portrait on the canvas.

So there was never any paint on his canvas
Until the people who lived in the buildings
Put him to work: "Try using the brush
As a means to an end. Select, for a portrait,
Something less angry and large, and more subject
To a painter's moods, or, perhaps, to a prayer."

How could he explain to them his prayer
That nature, not art, might usurp the canvas?

He chose his wife for a new subject,
Making her vast, like ruined buildings,
As if, forgetting itself, the portrait
Had expressed itself without a brush.

Slightly encouraged, he dipped his brush
In the sea, murmuring a heartfelt prayer:
"My soul, when I paint this next portrait
Let it be you who wrecks the canvas."
The news spread like wildfire through the buildings:
He had gone back to the sea for his subject.

Imagine a painter crucified by his subject!
Too exhausted even to lift his brush,
He provoked some artists leaning from the buildings
To malicious mirth: "We haven't a prayer
Now, of putting ourselves on canvas,
Or getting the sea to sit for a portrait!"

Others declared it a self-portrait.
Finally all indications of a subject
Began to fade, leaving the canvas
Perfectly white. He put down the brush.
At once a howl, that was also a prayer,
Arose from the overcrowded buildings.

They tossed him, the portrait, from the tallest of the
    buildings;
And the sea devoured the canvas and the brush
As though his subject had decided to remain a prayer.

JOHN ASHBERY

John Ashbery's poems usually start with a subject but then almost never go on to develop it or to take it in an expectable direction. His poems are, instead, full of just thinking, not thinking of the kind that necessarily leads to any conclusion, but the kind that goes in dreams and daydreams and other imaginings, in memories and in momentary perceptions, in the back of our minds, the kind that we are barely aware of, that seems almost to go on by itself. In John Ashbery's poetry this thinking is very sophisticated: it shows a knowledge of many things, an awareness of literature and of many styles of talking and writing. At one moment the poem may sound like someone talking on a bus, at another like an old work of literature or a book of philosophy, then like a comic strip or a popular song. Often the language is very simple, as the language of thinking and talking to oneself often is ("He is passing by. No, that other one,/Upstairs"), though surprising words come up, sentences are broken off, the subject changes, the tone changes. Most poets choose from all that's going on in their thoughts and organize it so as to say what they want to say. Ashbery, though, seems to leave it more the way it occurs, writing his poems more in the style that our minds work in when we're not really trying to make things follow or be logical. In fact, "making sense" is only one of the activities of our minds. There's a lot going on otherwise. One thing that poetry does is to make us more aware of the less obvious parts of our experience, and in that way it increases our understanding of ourselves and others.

In his poems, Ashbery makes an artistic order of the seeming disorder by the way he varies language and subject and tone, as well as by such formal devices as the sestina, for example, or beginning every line with the same word ("He").

He writes in a straightforward-sounding way, as if what he was saying made perfect sense and were perfectly clear. So when you read his poems you are often not ready for the pleasantly confusing experience it turns out to be. Maybe you even feel that you've somehow missed the point. Usually, there really isn't a point—at least, not the kind of point you might expect.

"He" is mysterious because some unnamed person seems very important. Every line of the poem tells something about him. Traditionally, the word *He* is used in this repeated ceremonial way only to refer to God or to Christ. But this "He" is obviously not a god. And we never do find out who he is. "Our Youth" seems to be an investigation into the meaning of youth, but the investigation doesn't seem to get very far. The last line says "the problem has not been solved," but it seems clear that a solution wasn't really the point, which was, instead, to be in the middle of the surprises and the mysteries of the problem—and the poem.

In Ashbery's poetry things are interesting just because they are there. These thought-of, dreamed-of, day-dreamed-of, or made-up things are put together in such a way that you see each one even if you don't know why you're looking at it. "The Instruction Manual" is not about a city the speaker knows, but about one he didn't see. He daydreams about it and gives a lot of very simple details, somewhat in the style of an elementary school report on a trip to Mexico. His daydream ends and he is back at work on his "instruction manual . . . on the uses of a new metal." We never know what the metal is, and more importantly, we never know what was the point of seeing all those people, streets, and colors in his daydream of Guadalajara. What did it mean? But the simple way that everything is seen and thought about in this poem is pleasant. As is often true in daydreams, the only things that happen are things you want to happen, and nothing is complicated. It is also rather like the way you see the obvious, superficial beauty of things when you are a tourist—here is the cathedral; look, there is a woman in a blue-and-white dress; here are the public gardens with the red-and-white flowers. It isn't usually possible to look at things this way: life is too complicated and involving—you're working for something, wanting something, having to figure something out. But when you travel, often it is possible to see the simple beauty of things without the usual interpretations and the usual concerns. And the sense you get of things then is a true one.

Write a poem about a place you imagine but haven't actually been to, or about a place that you saw long ago and liked, or perhaps about a place you've seen in pictures in a magazine, in a comic book, in a movie. Discover the place as you write, describing everything in the simple, superficial-seeming way John Ashbery writes about Guadalajara. Tell what color everything is, thinking about materials—cotton, mahogany, marble—and about shapes—round, slender, pointed. Tell what people, what flowers and trees, what churches and houses, are there, what the weather is like, what sounds and smells are in the air. Talk about anything in the city you want to, and in any order, as if there is nowhere in particular you have to get to, nothing of great importance to see. It may help to start lines with expressions like "Now we see," "Here there is," and "Over here on the left." If you like, write as if you are the voice in a travel movie or the writer of a guidebook. Or you can describe each new thing as if it were a new square of a comic book. Write in the present tense. Before you write each line, you might close your eyes and think of exactly what, in this city, you would like to do or see.

A form you might like to try is the sestina, of which Ashbery's "The Painter" is an example. There are six 6-line stanzas and a final stanza of only three lines. The idea is to end all the lines with one of the same six words. In the short last stanza, one of the words is at the end and in the middle of each of the three lines. These "end words" are repeated in a special order, which you can figure out from "The Painter" or by this formula: Imagine that the words are numbered 1, 2, 3, 4, 5, and 6. The order of their appearance in the various stanzas is as follows: first stanza, 1 2 3 4 5 6; second stanza, 6 1 5 2 4 3; third, 3 6 4 1 2 5; fourth, 5 3 2 6 1 4; fifth, 4 5 1 3 6 2; sixth, 2 4 6 5 3 1; seventh, 1 2 3 4 5 6. (Remember that in the seventh stanza one word is in the middle of the line and one at the end.)

This seems more complicated than it is. If you want to make it simpler, you can write down the end words of all your lines in advance. This form is a wonderful way of playing with different meanings of words and with different ways of using them. For end words, choose six words that for some reason or other you like, words that intrigue you, that you like to say. Or choose words that can be used in a lot of different ways. The poem will be much more fun to write if you let the end words inspire the line you write instead of trying to fit the end words into lines you've already written; that is, if the end word is *gate*, let the word *gate* suggest the line. If the next end word is *sleep*, let *sleep* suggest the next line, without your trying to make it go with the first line too much. Remember, each line doesn't have to be a sentence. The end word can be in the middle of a sentence. Try to use each word in a different way each time you use it. It may be that toward the middle of the poem a strange story or scene will begin to emerge. See what happens if you continue to let it go in its own direction. After you finish, you can go back and make it clearer if you wish.

The sestina was invented by a troubadour poet named Arnaut Daniel in the eleventh century. Many poets have tried this form. Dante, for instance, wrote a sestina. In our time, W. H. Auden and Ezra Pound, among others, have written good sestinas. Trying a new form is very good for your writing, if you think of it as an inspiration instead of as a limitation and allow it to lead you to say things you wouldn't otherwise say.

Gary Snyder
(1930–   )

FOUR POEMS FOR ROBIN

SIWASHING IT OUT ONCE
IN SIUSLAW FOREST

I slept under   rhododendron
All night   blossoms fell
Shivering on   a sheet of cardboard
Feet stuck   in my pack
Hands deep   in my pockets
Barely   able   to   sleep.
I remembered   when we were in school
Sleeping together   in a big warm bed
We were   the youngest lovers
When we broke up   we were still nineteen.
Now our   friends are married
You teach   school back east
I dont mind   living this way
Green hills   the long blue beach
But sometimes   sleeping in the open
I think back   when I had you.

A SPRING NIGHT IN
SHOKOKU-JI

Eight years ago this May
We walked under cherry blossoms
At night in an orchard in Oregon.
All that I wanted then
Is forgotten now, but you.
Here in the night
In a garden of the old capital
I feel the trembling ghost of Yugao
I remember your cool body
Naked under a summer cotton dress.

AN AUTUMN MORNING
IN SHOKOKU-JI

Last night watching the Pleiades,
Breath smoking in the moonlight,
Bitter memory like vomit
Choked my throat.
I unrolled a sleeping bag
On mats on the porch
Under thick autumn stars.
In dream you appeared
(Three times in nine years)
Wild, cold, and accusing.
I woke shamed and angry:
The pointless wars of the heart.
Almost dawn. Venus and Jupiter.
The first time I have
Ever seen them close.

DECEMBER AT YASE

You said, that October,
In the tall dry grass by the orchard
When you chose to be free,
"Again someday, maybe ten years."

After college I saw you
One time. You were strange.
And I was obsessed with a plan.

Now ten years and more have
Gone by: I've always known
        where you were—
I might have gone to you
Hoping to win your love back.
You still are single.

I didn't.
I thought I must make it alone. I
Have done that.

Only in dream, like this dawn,
Does the grave, awed intensity
Of our young love
Return to my mind, to my flesh.

We had what the others
All crave and seek for;
We left it behind at nineteen.

I feel ancient, as though I had
Lived many lives.

And may never now know
If I am a fool
Or have done what my
      karma demands.

AUGUST ON SOURDOUGH,
A VISIT FROM DICK BREWER

You hitched a thousand miles
      north from San Francisco
Hiked up the mountainside   a mile in the air
The little cabin—one room—
      walled in glass
Meadows and snowfields,   hundreds of peaks.
We lay in our sleeping bags
      talking half the night;
Wind in the guy-cables   summer mountain rain.
Next morning I went with you
      as far as the cliffs.
Loaned you my poncho—   the rain across the shale—
You down the snowfield
      flapping in the wind
Waving a last goodbye   half hidden in the clouds
To go on hitching
      clear to New York;
Me back to my mountain   and far, far, west.

WHY LOG TRUCK DRIVERS RISE EARLIER THAN STUDENTS OF ZEN

In the high seat, before-dawn dark,
Polished hubs gleam
And the shiny diesel stack
Warms and flutters
Up the Tyler Road grade
To the logging on Poorman creek.
Thirty miles of dust.

There is no other life.

GARY SNYDER

Gary Snyder's poems suggest a certain kind of life: simple, out-of-doors, usually in nature rather than in the city, a life of camping out, hitchhiking, of hard work with one's hands, and most often of being alone: alone driving a truck at dawn, alone sleeping outside and thinking about a girl he once loved, alone looking out the window, alone in a little house in the mountains thinking about a friend. In such a life, it seems, you are more likely to have time for what's really important to you—time for the simple awareness of what it is to be alive, time to see what your own life is like, time to know what things really mean to you, the people, the beauty all around you, the continual changes. Gary Snyder's poems seem to have that kind of awareness.

He often writes poems that are short and simple. He says very little about what he feels; he says more about the place and about what has happened. His poems seem sometimes almost like notes, notes that just say the main things and leave out everything that is unnecessary. It is like the way one thinks and remembers when there is no one to convince, no one to explain anything to, not even oneself.

It is usually hard for people to write directly and simply about their own lives. While you are still in the middle of what is happening, you may see things the way you want them to be rather than the way they really are. Or very momentary feelings may seem overwhelmingly important—your nervousness, your wishes, your discomfort. On the other hand, when you're writing about something that is in the past, you may want to analyze it or explain it or, without realizing it, start to rearrange it so that your feelings about it are more bearable or so that it makes more sense. Whether something is in the present or in the past, a lot can seem to be at stake—your idea of yourself, the way you want to see yourself—when you write about your own life. And that can influence what you write.

For one thing, the details that are important to you are sometimes quite different from the ones you might think should be important. Sometimes when you remember something, you suddenly know the things that matter to you. They can be surprisingly simple—like the kind of dress the girl had on in "A Spring Night in Shokoku-ji." Probably at the time of the visit described in "August on Sourdough," the two friends were very involved in what they said to each other when they stayed up half the night talking. But what Gary Snyder remembers is not what they said, but how long they talked. What you care about is often different from what you would have expected. Think about what happens when you remember someone. You see a certain look, a certain shirt or dress, remember the name of someone else you knew at that time, hear a few words spoken at a certain door or on a certain street in a certain kind of weather. The things you remember may have happened on different days and do not seem in any way connected, until a feeling suddenly connects them—maybe you don't know why. In Gary Snyder's poems, he is writing about the past or the present, that is the way the details seem to be connected—by strong, clear feelings that he doesn't necessarily talk about or explain or analyze or regret. He writes about what is there, and about what was there, without change or addition. That is part of what gives his poems, along with the strong emotions, the feeling of strength, even toughness—and the sense of time—of having had things, then lost them, while everything continued to go on.

Write a poem about something in the past—about a person you once loved, a place, a certain time. Maybe you don't really know why that particular time still seems so important to you. Let the poem be mainly details—perhaps one in every line—about what you are doing now and what you remember from then. You might try using a number of sentences, some about the present, some about the past, making each one brief and simple, beginning with such words as "You said," "I think," "You wore," "It was," and so on. Don't use the word *remember* —your memories may seem more present if you don't. It is possible to get the feelings you have about the time into your poem without ever saying how you feel. Trust the details of the poem to show what you feel. Or if you say what you feel, say it simply—there is no one to convince. The idea is not to explain your life, but rather to get a sense of it, how it is and was, into the poem. You might try writing as if you were taking notes. Don't be afraid of leaving things out—there are other poems to write. One way of isolating the details of the poem, making them more like notes, is to leave spaces in the middle of lines, as Gary Snyder sometimes does.

LeRoi Jones
(Imamu Amiri Baraka)
(1934 –   )

COLD TERM

All the things. The objects.
Cold freeze of the park, while
passing. People there. White inside
outside on horses trotting ignorantly
There is so much pain for our blackness
so much beauty there, if we think to what
our beautiful selves would make
of the world, steaming turning blackouts
over cold georgia, the spirits hover
waiting for the world to arrive at ecstasy.
Why cant we love each other and be beautiful?
Why do the beautiful corner each other and spit
poison? Why do the beautiful not hangout together
and learn to do away with evil? Why are the beautiful
not living together and feeling each other's trials?
Why are the beautiful not walking with their arms around
each other laughing softly at the soft laughter of black
        beauty?
Why are the beautiful dreading each other, and hiding
        from
each other? Why are the beautiful sick and divided
like myself?

BALLAD OF THE MORNING STREETS

The magic of the day is the morning
I want to say the day is morning high
and sweet, good
morning.

The ballad of the morning streets, sweet
voices turns
of cool warm weather
high around the early windows grey to blue
and down again amongst the kids and
broken signs, is pure love magic, sweet day
come into me, let me live with you
and dig your blazing

SONG FORM

Morning uptown, quiet on the street,
no matter the distinctions that can be
made, quiet, very quiet, on the street.
Sun's not even up, just some kid and me,
skating, both of us, at the early sun, and
amazed there is grace for us, without our
having to smile too tough, or be very pleasant
even to each other. Merely to be mere, ly to be

RED LIGHT

The only thing we know is the thing
we turn out to be, I don't care what
you think, its true, now you think
your way out of this

AIR

I am lost in hot fits
of myself
trying
to get
out. Lost
because
I am kinder
to myself
than I
need
Softer
w/ others
than is good
for them.

Taller
than
most/
Stronger
What is it
about me

that
frightens me
loses
me
tosses me helplessly
in
the air.

Oh love
Songs
dont leave
w/o me
that you
are the weakness
of my simplicity

Are feeling
& want
All need
& romance
I wd do anything
to be loved
& this
is a stupid
mistake.

A POEM FOR BLACK HEARTS

For Malcolm's eyes, when they broke
the face of some dumb white man. For
Malcolm's hands raised to bless us

all black and strong in his image
of ourselves. For Malcolm's words
fire darts, the victor's tireless
thrusts, words hung above the world
change as it may, he said it, and
for this he was killed, for saying,
and feeling, and being/change, all
collected hot in his heart, For Malcolm's
heart, raising us above our filthy cities,
for his stride, and his beat, and his address
to the gray monsters of the world. For Malcolm's
pleas for your dignity, black men, for your life,
black man, for the filling of your minds
with righteousness. For all of him dead and
gone and vanished from us, and all of him which
clings to our speech black god of our time.
For all of him, and all of yourself, look up,
black man, quit stuttering and shuffling, look up,
black man, quit whining and stooping, for all of him,
For Great Malcolm a prince of the earth, let nothing in
        us rest
until we avenge ourselves for his death, stupid animals
that killed him, let us never breathe a pure breath if
we fail and white men call us faggots till the end of
the earth.

LEROI JONES (IMAMU AMIRI BARAKA)

When LeRoi Jones was thirty-four years old, he changed his name to Imamu Amiri Baraka, saying his old name was a "slave name." The new, Islamic name had nothing to do with, and was part of his separating himself from, the White American culture he wished to reject. At the same time, his poetry changed. His early poems are often rather impressionistic, witty, sensitive poems with short lines, poems about what it feels like to be young, excited, part of the avant-garde art scene in New York, in and out of love. In his mid-thirties, however, a new kind of awareness of what it meant to be Black and of the all-importance of the problems of Black people seemingly overwhelmed everything else in his life and in his poetry. That is when he changed his name. His poems became poems about Black people, or pleas to Black people, or prophecies or threats connected with them, or poems about himself somewhat as before, but often with a more somber tone and with more consciousness of himself as a Black poet.

To be a political poet, a poet with a cause, is in one way wonderful and inspiring. You have a theme you believe in, strong feelings, a reason to write. In another way it is difficult if you want to be a good poet. Attitudes, convictions, beliefs, however right they are, do not necessarily make good poetry. Usually in political writing you figure out in advance what you are going to say (and feel); it is fixed and consistent, and in accord with certain agreed-upon positions. This means not having much room to discover anything as you write; and, often, saying things that other people have already said; and not being able to say all that you could say. The problem in writing poetry about a cause is how to remain yourself, how to be personal enough so that your own thoughts and feelings can get into the poem—feelings which may be contradictory and which may include questions and doubts—how to be free enough to remain open to inspiration and original perceptions.

Suppose you are not making a political speech or writing a battle song but are simply very engrossed by and absorbed in a political cause that means more to you than anything else in your life. And suppose that you write a poem, any poem, inspired, as poems usually are, by what you're feeling and doing at the time; and no matter where you begin—looking out the window, talking to someone, taking a walk—this cause is there, and is the main thing in your feelings and in your thoughts. This is what a poem by LeRoi Jones such as "Cold Term" is like. His cause, his theme, is obviously his main inspiration. But the poem isn't limited to that: he looks at different things; he feels different things; he is filled with longing, anger, excitement, sadness, doubt, love.

In the first part of "Cold Term" the poet looks at things around him in the city in the winter—objects, the frozen park, people, some people on horses (perhaps policemen)—and this whole world of the city with its white people and its winter whiteness makes him think of the suffering of Black people. Then, immediately, he thinks of how beautiful Black people are, what "beautiful selves" they have, what wonderful things they could do, what a good world they could make, a beautiful and ecstatic world, if only they could love each other and act toward each other in a beautiful way. The rest of the poem is one question after another about why Black people don't do this. He doesn't seem to expect an answer. The questions are mainly statements of the way things are, and they seem more sad than angry. At the end there is a sort of answer: he himself is "sick and divided" and so are all Black people, and that is why they don't do what they could do. The poem is about an ideal, a beautiful ideal, and about how hard it is to achieve it. It says things that a political speech couldn't say.

The cause LeRoi Jones writes about is a great and serious one, and he is very dedicated to it. Of course, not everyone is a member, as he is, of a group to whom so much harm has been done by others; and not everyone in such a group feels the harm done to him and to others so strongly. But everyone cares about something, about some situation that involves other people and needs to be changed. It may be being Black, being a woman, being a student, being Mexican American, being the age you are, living where you live. Think of something of this kind that you really care about and write about it. Let your feelings about it be at the center of what you say, but don't make an oration. Talk as you talk to your friends or to yourself. Let yourself discover what your ideas and feelings really are as you go along. Start anywhere—with what you see when you look out the window or when you take a walk—and tell about things as they occur to you. Don't worry too much about staying on the subject—if your feeling is strong, probably everything you say will be connected in some way or another.

Kenneth Koch
(1925 –   )

LUNCH

The lanternslides grinding out B-flat minor
Chords to the ears of the deaf youngster who sprays in
   Hicksville
The sides of a car with the dream-splitting paint
Of pianos (he dreamt of one day cutting the Conserva-
   tory
In two with his talent), these lanternslides, I say,
They are— The old woman hesitated. A lifesaver was
   shoved down her throat; then she continued:
They are some very good lanternslides in that bunch.
   Then she fainted
And we revived her with flowers. She smiled sleepily at
   the sun.
He is my own boy, she said, with her glass hand falling
   through the sparkling red America of lunch.

That old boilermaker she has in her back yard.
Olaf said, used to be her sweetheart years back.
One day, though, a train passed, and pressed her hard.
And she deserted life and love for liberty.
We carried Olaf softly into the back yard
And laid him down with his head under the steamroller.
Then Jill took the wheel and I tinkered with the engine,

Till we rolled him under, rolled him under the earth.
When people ask us what's in our back yard
Now, we don't like to tell them, Jill says, laying her silver
    bandannaed head on my greened bronze shoulder.
Then we both dazzle ourselves with the red whiteness of
    lunch.

That old woman named Tessie Runn
Had a tramp boyfriend who toasted a bun.
They went to Florida, but Maxine Schweitzer was hard
    of
Hearing and the day afterwards the judge adjourned the
    trial.
When it finally came for judgment to come up
Of delicious courtyards near the Pantheon,
At last we had to let them speak, the children whom
    flowers had made statues
For the rivers of water which came from their funnel;
And we stood there in the middle of existence
Dazzled by the white paraffin of lunch.

Music in Paris and water coming out from the flannel
Of the purist person galloping down the Madeleine
Toward a certain wafer. Hey! just a minute! the sunlight
    is being rifled
By the green architecture of the flowers. But the boule-
    vard turned a big blue deaf ear
Of cinema placards to the detonated traveler. He had
    forgotten the blue defilade of lunch!

Genoa! a stone's throw from Acapulco
If an engine were built strong enough.
And down where the hulls and scungilli,
Glisteningly unconscious, agree,
I throw a game of shoes with Horace Sturnbul
And forget to eat lunch.

O launch, lunch, you dazzling hoary tunnel
To paradise!
Do you see that snowman tackled over there
By summer and the sea? A boardwalk went to Istanbul
And back under his left eye. We saw the Moslems praying
In Rhodes. One had a red fez, another had a black cap.
And in the extended heat of afternoon,
As an ice-cold gradual sweat covered my whole body,
I realized, and the carpet swam like a red world at my feet
In which nothing was green, and the Moslems went on
      praying,
That we had missed lunch, and a perpetual torrent
    roared into the sea
Of my understanding. An old woman gave us bread and
    rolls on the street.

The dancing wagon has come! here is the dancing
    wagon!
Come up and get lessons—here is lemonade and gram-
    mar!
Here is drugstore and cowboy—all that is America—plus
    sex, perfumes, and shimmers—all the Old World;
Come and get it—and here is your reading matter
For twenty-nine centuries, and here finally is lunch—
To be served in the green defilade under the roaring
    tower
Where Portugal meets Spain inside a flowered made-
    leine.

My ginger dress has nothing on, but yours
Has on a picture of Queen Anne Boleyn
Surrounded by her courtiers eating lunch
And on the back a one of Henry the Eighth
Summoning all his courtiers in for lunch.

And the lunchboat has arrived
From Spain.

Everyone getting sick is on it;
The bold people and the sadists are on it;
I am glad I am not on it,
I am having a big claw of garlic for lunch—
But it plucks me up in the air,
And there, above the ship, on a cloud
I see the angels eating lunch.
One has a beard, another a moustache,
And one has some mustard smeared on his ears.
A couple of them ask me if I want to go to Honolulu,
And I accept—it's all right—
Another time zone: we'll be able to have lunch.
They are very beautiful and transparent,
My two traveling companions,
And they will go very well with Hawaii
I realize as we land there,
That dazzling red whiteness—it is our desire . . .
For whom? The angels of lunch.

Oh I sat over a glass of red wine
And you came out dressed in a paper cup.
An ant-fly was eating hay-mire in the chair-rafters
And large white birds flew in and dropped edible animals
        to the ground.
If they had been gulls it would have been garbage
Or fish. We have to be fair to the animal kingdom,
But if I do not wish to be fair, if I wish to eat lunch
Undisturbed—? The light of day shines down. The world
        continues.

We stood in the little hutment in Biarritz
Waiting for lunch, and your hand clasped mine
And I felt it was sweaty;
And then lunch was served,
Like the bouquet of an enchantress.
Oh the green whites and red yellows
And purple whites of lunch!

The bachelor eats his lunch,
The married man eats his lunch,
And old Uncle Joris belches
The seascape in which a child appears
Eating a watermelon and holding a straw hat.
He moves his lips as if to speak
But only sea air emanates from this childish beak.
It is the moment of sorrows.
And in the shores of history,
Which stretch in both directions, there are no happy
    tomorrows.
But Uncle Joris holds his apple up and begins to speak
To the child. Red waves fan my universe with the green
    macaw of lunch.

This street is deserted;
I think my eyes are empty;
Let us leave
Quickly.
Day bangs on the door and is gone.

Then they picked him up and carried him away from that
    company.
When he awoke he was in the fire department, and sleepy
    but not tired.
They gave him a hoseful of blue Spain to eat for lunch,
And Portugal was waiting for him at the door, like a
    rainstorm of evening raspberries.

It is time to give lunch to my throat and not my chest.
What? either the sting ray has eaten my lunch
Or else—and she searches the sky for something else;
But I am far away, seeming blue-eyed, empirical . . .

Let us give lunch to the lunch—
But how shall we do it?
The headwaiters expand and confer;

289 · Kenneth Koch

Will little pieces of cardboard box do it?
And what about silver and gold pellets?
The headwaiters expand and confer:
And what if the lunch should refuse to eat anything at all?
Why then we'd say be damned to it.
And the red doorway would open on a green railway
And the lunch would be put in a blue car
And it would go away to Whippoorwill Valley
Where it would meet and marry Samuel Dogfoot, and
    bring forth seven offspring,
All of whom would be half human, half lunch;
And when we saw them, sometimes, in the gloaming,
We would take off our mining hats and whistle Tweet
    twee-oo,
With watering mouths staring at the girls in pink organdy
    frocks,
Not realizing they really were half edible,
And we would die still without knowing it;
So to prevent anything happening that terrible
Let's give everybody we see and like a good hard bite
    right now,
To see what they are, because it's time for lunch!

KENNETH KOCH

Poets are usually not objective about their own work, but of course they know things about it that no one else does. What they say can give you another way to look at it. What I say about my poem "Lunch" is a combination of what I thought and felt while I was writing it and what I thought about it afterward.

I wrote "Lunch" in 1958, in eastern Long Island, in one afternoon, on the typewriter. I changed it very little after I wrote it. There was no single event at the time that inspired it. However, not too long before I wrote it, I had been in Europe for a year and had eaten lunch in many different cities and countries, some lunches in beautiful places, often in strange ones. Always in the midst of seeing cathedrals and paintings and statues, walking around cities thinking of the past and present at the same time, in the midst of whatever I was doing, there would be, at a certain moment, lunch. When I was traveling, lunch was not something I would have expected to inspire me to write a poem. While I was writing this poem, though, the idea of lunch—or maybe partly just the word *lunch*—seemed to become a way of connecting a lot of different feelings and sensations—from my travels and elsewhere. I think probably the seeming lack of importance and poeticalness of lunch (compared, say, to the ocean, history, love, cathedrals, and so on) made me like using it, as did the rather funny and slightly dissonant sound of the word.

Some details in the poem are closely connected to particular moments in my travels—in my mind, at least. Others are connected to my childhood, to books, to all kinds of experiences. The whole poem seems to me in certain ways like traveling. It is always changing places, and it is always beginning a new story or part of a story which seems unconnected to what happened before.

This disconnectedness and always starting over again were things that, when I traveled, I had liked. I liked them also when I was writing. In my poem I was traveling not only from city to city (Paris, Genoa, Athens, Istanbul) but also from story to story and from style to style. I kept changing my way of writing in the poem—sometimes using rhyme and sometimes not; sometimes being very poetical, sometimes prosey; sometimes being realistic, sometimes fantastic. I never knew what was going to come next in the poem. I wanted to let myself be surprised by what I was writing—this, too, was a little bit like travel, like being in a strange city and, for no reason, deciding to walk down a particular street or to go into a certain doorway.

I remember that while I was writing "Lunch," I was quite excited and felt that I was doing something new and something that I liked. The poem, it seems to me, was at least partly about the dazzlingness of things and their beauty and breathtakingness and craziness, and about there being so much that is always going on and so many changes. This sense of things was not something I understood or was even clearly conscious of, so I couldn't have planned a poem about it if I'd wanted to; it was just something I felt at certain moments. It felt important to me, though, and serious—the funniness and the unconnectedness were part of that.

I wrote other poems in the late fifties, in somewhat the same style, though of course not on exactly the same theme as this one. The poems I've written recently resemble them, I think, in some ways but not in others. Poets, if they write over a period of years, often write differently at different times.

To write a poem like "Lunch," I suppose you could begin by finding a word or phrase like *lunch* to keep repeating—it could be *water*, *sweetheart*, *train*, *clouds*, *breakfast*, *bedroom*, any one of a number of things; then you could think of different places, try different styles of writing, start a different story every few lines; you can make it a rule that the stories have no connection with each other except for the repeated word or phrase. Start your stories at the beginning, in the middle, anyplace. One way to keep the stories from being too connected is to imagine you are starting the poem all over again with each one.

A Note to Teachers

This book is meant to be self-explanatory for students, but there are a few additional things about reading and writing poetry that seem worth saying to those who teach them.

Reading the poems in this book will help students with their writing of poetry, and this writing will help them with their reading. It's important that students feel comfortable about reading poetry, that they be able to read it with pleasure and get from it whatever they can. The understanding of a poem is more likely to show up first as feeling something rather than as knowing something—the student may be moved by the poem, excited or inspired by it before he knows much else about it. Because this is different from what happens in other academic subjects, it is sometimes hard to realize that this first response is a serious one and a real part of learning. But in poetry it is. The first sign of knowing is usually liking something in the poem: a tone, an attitude, certain words, sounds, kinds of subjects. Students profit most from teaching that recognizes this and that helps them to feel close to poetry, not overwhelmed by its problems and liking whatever it makes them think and feel.

The essays in this book are meant to be that kind of

teaching, and class discussion along the same lines would probably be the most helpful kind. Probably because teachers themselves often feel uncomfortable with poetry, a poem is sometimes taught as if it were a thorny problem that had to be faced and dealt with—as if the important thing were to get to the bottom of it, to solve all its mysteries, to analyze everything until all was understood. Although poetry is, in a way, complex, knowing everything about a poem isn't the point for beginning readers—and indeed for most nonscholarly readers. And since poetry isn't purely intellectual, if it is taught as if it were, it will simply never make any real sense.

Just going a little way is a fine beginning and can have significant results. If a student feels relaxed about poetry, and if he likes something in a poet's work, he will probably use that in his own poems, and from so doing, he will come back to the poems of others a more perceptive reader. And this process goes on. If poetry is made to seem mysteriously complex and distant from the student, the process won't have a chance to begin.

Students are usually beginning writers and beginning readers of poetry, and the best things a teacher can do for them are to praise and appreciate what they write and to encourage them to write more. It's important for them to experiment in their writing, to try all kinds of things. What they write may be uneven: something moving and surprising on one day, something relatively flat and conventional the next day. Just as likely is variation inside the same poem—one part clearly better than another. All this is perfectly natural. Also, a student's talent for writing may be hard to recognize at first. For one thing, the first poems he writes may not be very good—they may be wild or sentimental or jokey—or he may write very little. Also, his talent probably won't be predictable from how well he is doing in other subjects.

Students not doing well in academic subjects may, with the right kind of encouragement, write poetry very well. It is a mistake to think poetry is something mainly for gifted students. Poetry can turn out to be very important to a student with a learning problem, for instance. The writing of less sophisticated students may be awkward at first, but after a while they too will write well. Whatever is good in what any student writes should be praised. Writing poetry in a classroom means taking chances— writing about your feelings, your ideas, your memories. The experience of doing so should be made as pleasant and as unthreatening as it can be. Praise of what is good shows you a direction in which to go. Negative criticism leaves you nowhere and, for most students, will do harm and no good. The rare student who has been writing a lot and feels the need for that kind of criticism will ask for it.

Everything about student poetry writing suggests that it is best not to give grades for it: the need for encouragement, the bad effects of adverse criticism, the need to feel free to try different things, the expectable unevenness of what is written. There is another reason too, a very important one, why grading can be injurious to the development of creative talent. To write poetry, one has to trust one's most personal and private responses to words and feelings and also one's judgment of what is good writing. Without trusting oneself in this way, one can't hope to arrive at the very individual kinds of discoveries that make poetry so much worth reading and worth writing. Grading is an impediment to this kind of artistic self-trust and self-reliance. To be rewarded by a good grade, the student may, consciously or not, begin writing to please the teacher, writing to satisfy standards other than his own, the only ones that can be of any use to him as an artist. The pleasure of writing things that you like is the best motivation for writing well. The students' own standards for their work, their own taste and sophistication and skill, get better as a result of writing a lot, reading and being influenced by the work of other poets, hearing their own work and the work of their classmates read aloud and appreciated. All this is inspiring. The idea in teaching poetry writing isn't to separate the good writers from the bad writers, but to give everyone a chance to write poetry as well as he can.

What is good in a poem, or in any creative work, will not be the same as what is good in a piece of expository writing. The objective of expository writing, whether its subject is facts or feelings, is to communicate what it has to say clearly, according to recognized standards of clarity. This means, among other things, its being well-organized, precise in its choice of words and its manner of saying things, and correct in its grammar, syntax, and punctuation. To know how to write this way is of immense importance for students socially, professionally, and personally. Writing poetry has other rewards, is another kind of writing, and of course is judged in a different way. With an expository essay, an appropriate first question is, "Can I understand it?" With a poem (or a story), you ask, "Is it beautiful? Is it new? Is it moving?" A creative work can sometimes be better for having broken the rules of clear exposition. Eliot's "The Love Song of J. Alfred Prufrock" has a nonrational organization, based on the momentary feelings of the protagonist, and this makes it a more moving poem than it would otherwise be. The total lack of punctuation in Apollinaire's poem "Zone" helps give it its artistically valuable quality of rapid movement through time and space. Expository writing develops clear thinking and clear, objective expression. Writing poetry develops the imaginative intelligence. It can give a student ease in expressing his feelings, attentiveness and sensitivity to words, and artistic or aesthetic appreciation of language and of how things are said. It can help him to bring together his feelings with what he learns and knows, give him a sense of accomplishment, a heightened sense of his own individual style, and a love of literature. It can help him to be aware of and able to use his own perceptiveness and originality in whatever he does. Like expository writing, it can be of great value in his education and in his life.

To develop his ability as a creative writer, the student has to feel free to write whatever words occur to him, to express his own view of things, to feel free to speak of his feelings without fear of being embarrassed or of being criticized for what he says. Feeling free this way is necessary because writing poetry is not primarily a description of something already existing, but a discovery, a creation of something new—made up of memories, thoughts, feelings, perceptions and, of course, words—which the writer to some degree finds as he goes along, while he is writing. If he doesn't feel free and comfortable when he writes, a great part of what he could say will be closed to him. He'll be afraid, or at least cautious, not a good or useful way to feel while writing a poem or, for that matter, while making a sketch or improvising a dance. It's important, then, for the teacher to know how it feels to be writing a poem and to give his students the sense that he knows what poetry is like, and that he takes pleasure in it, as they do.

SOME PRACTICAL SUGGESTIONS

Since you don't want to grade the students' poems, one possibility, if some grading arrangement has to be made, is to give a grade entirely on the basis of the students' having written the poems. Explain in advance that if someone writes all the poems, he gets an A, adding, of course, that anyone who has trouble writing the poems can consult with you and be helped. Sometimes fear of being made fun of, embarrassment about spelling, or some other difficult feeling may make a student unable or unwilling to write, and you can help with this.

The first few poems should probably be written in class, where there is a sort of equality—of time available in which to write, of everyone doing the same thing, of your being there to help if wanted—and lack of distraction. Once students get used to writing, they may like writing at home as well, or at least taking home and finishing what they began in school. Some kinds of poems—one in the style of "Thirteen Ways of Looking at a Blackbird," for example—may not be manageable in one class. Students could take their poems home or spend a second or even a third class on them.

When asking students to write, tell them that they have the option of not having their poems read aloud or mimeographed, that they can write on their poems, "Please do not read aloud," or "Please do not mimeograph." This possibility of remaining anonymous makes people feel freer in what they write. When they begin to have confidence in their poetry, and when they hear that of others being liked and praised, they rarely request this kind of privacy. When you read the poems out loud, it's best not to read the students' names until they want you to. It's best if the response to the students' poems takes place in class, with your reading the poems aloud appreciatively or with the students reading their own. Often there isn't enough time for everyone's poem to be read; in such cases some poems should be read, and then, the next time this happens, poems by other students should be read. The very best situation is hearing all the poems in each class, whenever that is possible.

If you feel unsure about what is good in a poem, just respond to what you like for whatever reason—the sound, the way a certain word is used, a surprising comparison, and so on. No intellectual explanation, of course, is necessary.

It is probably important in expository writing that the students concentrate a lot on revising and perfecting what they write, since the object is to communicate something logically and clearly. But in poetry it is probably not too important if your students don't write what you would consider to be finished works. A student can learn more from writing several lines that are original and good and surprising than from writing a rather ordinary poem that is very polished and complete.

When you're talking about a student's poem, be sure that you're talking about the poem and not about the student. That is, it is better to say, "This poem is sad," than it is to say, "Tim, I didn't realize you were so sad." If he gets the feeling that the teacher is more interested in the emotional content than in the poetry, the student may become embarrassed and inhibited and avoid writing about what he really cares about.

Give everyone's poems equal attention. Just as everyone's work should be in the magazine or mimeographed book, so everyone's poems should be, at some point, on the bulletin board, and everyone should read his work aloud, in class or at a reading in the auditorium, if there is one.

If not all the poems are read aloud in class, it's good to collect them all and read them for yourself. It is best not to make any marks or comments on them, however. You can tell your students you want to read their poems and just give them back the next day.

It's a good idea for students to keep the poems they write in a special folder or notebook. This gives them a chance to read their own poems over, to be heartened by them, to be influenced by them, to change them if they like.

Spelling, punctuation, neatness, and other such matters have nothing to do with writing poetry well. If students have to think about them while writing, it's likely to interfere with their inspiration, with the free flow of ideas, feelings, and words. Errors and unclear handwriting can always be corrected later.

Mimeographing or otherwise duplicating the students' poems so that they can read one another's (and their own) work may be wonderfully inspiring. If it can't be done every lesson or so, then a sort of duplicated poetry magazine or collection once a term is certainly worthwhile. Every student's work should be represented. If it's a once-a-term publication, students should choose which poem of theirs to include.

It is natural for high school students to be concerned with sexual feelings and with aggressive ones, and natural for them to express these sometimes in what they write. You might explain, if this becomes a problem, that you want to read everything the students write, but that if you think any poem will hurt or upset anyone in the class, you won't read it aloud; or if you think it won't bother the class but is likely to seriously bother students' families, you won't mimeograph it.

Everyone should have a chance to write poetry. A few students will already be interested in it, but most will never have had the chance to know that they could do it. It would be a mistake to continue this separation. Those who haven't yet written may write poetry well and like it.

Students with learning disabilities may be very good at writing poetry. So may students with psychological or social problems. Writing often gives confidence to students which they haven't been able to get from other parts of their education.

Detailed discussion of poetic form and rhetorical devices is likely to put students off, and they don't need to know about them in order to write well and to read and understand poetry. If knowledge of such matters is required for a particular test or exam, teach it separately from writing. Of course, if a student asks about alliteration or the sonnet form, it's fine to talk about it.

Biographies

WALT WHITMAN (1819–1892) was born in Huntington, Long Island, New York. In 1855, when he was thirty-six, he published the first edition of his book of poems, *Leaves of Grass*. Throughout his life after that, he went on writing and adding poems to the book. "Song of Myself" was in the first, 1855, edition.

EMILY DICKINSON (1830–1886) was born in Amherst, Massachusetts, and went on living there. Though she wrote a great many poems, she published very few of them during her lifetime. After her death, over a thousand of her poems were found in her desk and published.

GERARD MANLEY HOPKINS (1844–1889), born in Essex in England and educated at Oxford, was a Jesuit priest. He didn't publish his poems, and they were known only to a few friends till a collection of them was published in 1918, almost thirty years after his death.

ARTHUR RIMBAUD (1854–1891) was born in Charleville, France. He began writing poetry when he was very young. He wrote most of his poems in verse between the ages of fifteen and nineteen and the prose poems in *The Illuminations* when he was about twenty. Shortly after that, he stopped writing poetry.

WILLIAM BUTLER YEATS (1865–1939) was an Irish poet, born near Dublin. He wrote plays as well as poetry and was a leading figure in the Irish literary renaissance of the twentieth century.

GERTRUDE STEIN (1874–1946), born in Pennsylvania, lived most of her life in Paris. She was part of a group of writers and painters that included Picasso, Matisse, and Ernest Hemingway. She wrote novels, poetry, and plays, and an autobiography, *The Autobiography of Alice B. Toklas.*

RAINER MARIA RILKE (1875–1926) was a German poet who was born in Prague, Czechoslovakia. Many of his poems, like "Childhood," were inspired by paintings or sculpture. He also wrote works in prose, among them *Letters to a Young Poet,* about being a poet and writing poetry.

WALLACE STEVENS (1879–1955), born in Reading, Pennsylvania, lived in Hartford, Connecticut, where he was president of an insurance company. His first book, *Harmonium,* was published when he was forty-four years old.

GUILLAUME APOLLINAIRE (1880–1918) lived and wrote in Paris. He wrote plays, novels, opera librettos, and art criticism, as well as poetry.

WILLIAM CARLOS WILLIAMS (1883–1963) was born in Rutherford, New Jersey. After studying medicine in America and in Germany, he came back to Rutherford and worked as a pediatrician. He wrote novels, short stories, and plays, as well as poetry.

D . H . LAWRENCE (1885–1930) was born in Nottingham, England. He wrote poetry, novels, short stories, and books about his travels to Mexico, Sardinia, and other places.

EZRA POUND (1885–1972), born in Hailey, Idaho, lived most of his life in Rapallo, Italy. Along with his short poems, his translations, and his critical works, he also wrote *The Cantos,* a poem hundreds of pages long, which he worked on for many years.

T . S . ELIOT (1888–1965), born in St. Louis, Missouri, lived most of his life in London. He wrote plays and criticism as well as poetry. He received the Nobel prize for literature in 1948.

VLADIMIR MAYAKOWSKY (1893–1930) lived in Moscow during the Russian Revolution and the first years of the new Soviet government. Along with his other poetry, he wrote political "poster poems" for the state, as well as several plays. "A Cloud in Trousers" was written in 1915, two years before the revolution, when Mayakowsky was associated with an avant-garde literary and artistic movement called Futurism.

E . E . CUMMINGS (1894–1962) was born in Cambridge, Massachusetts, went to Harvard, drove an ambulance in World War I, lived in Paris and after that mostly in New York.

FEDERICO GARCÍA LORCA (1899–1936) was born in Spain and lived most of his life there, in An-

dalusia. He wrote plays as well as poetry. At the begin-
ning of the Spanish Civil War, he was shot by soldiers of
Franco's army.

W . H . A U D E N (1907–1973) was born in York, Eng-
land, and educated at Oxford. In the 1930's he was part
of a group of British poets (of whom others were Ste-
phen Spender, Louis MacNeice, and Cecil Day Lewis)
who wrote in a new way about the modern world. In 1939
he moved to New York City, where he lived for most of
the rest of his life. He wrote plays and criticism as well
as poetry.

A L L E N G I N S B E R G (1926–   ), born in Paterson,
New Jersey, and educated at Columbia University, now
lives in Boulder, Colorado. In the 1950's he was a princi-
pal figure in various literary and cultural movements,
among them those known as the San Francisco Renais-
sance and the Beat Generation, and since that time has
continued to be an active force in cultural and political
causes.

F R A N K O ' H A R A (1926–1966) was born in Baltimore,
educated at Harvard, and lived in New York City. He
wrote plays and art criticism as well as poetry. He was
killed in an automobile accident when he was forty.

J O H N A S H B E R Y (1927–   ), born in Rochester,
New York, and educated at Harvard, has lived since then
in Paris and New York. He is a playwright and an art critic
as well as a poet.

G A R Y S N Y D E R (1930–   ), born in San Francisco,
lived for a number of years in Japan, where he became
a Zen Buddhist. He now lives in California. He has been
an active participant in ecological causes.

LEROI JONES (1934–   ), also known as Imamu Baraka, was born in Newark, New Jersey, and educated at Howard University. A political activist, he was, in 1972, one of the leaders of the National Black Political Caucus. He writes plays and essays as well as poetry.

Index

ABOUT THE AUTHORS

KENNETH KOCH's books of poetry include *The Burning Mystery of Anna in 1951*; *The Duplications*; *The Art of Love*; *The Pleasures of Peace*; *Thank You and Other Poems*; and *Ko, or a Season on Earth*. He is also the author of a book of plays, *A Change of Hearts*; a novel, *The Red Robins*; and three books on education— *Wishes, Lies and Dreams*; *Rose, Where Did You Get That Red?*; and *I Never Told Anybody*. He lives in New York City and is professor of English at Columbia University.

KATE FARRELL has published her poetry in *Poetry*, *Partisan Review*, *New York Arts Journal*, and other magazines. She teaches poetry writing in the New York poets-in-the-schools program, and collaborated with Kenneth Koch on the research for and writing of *I Never Told Anybody*. She lives in New York City.